Breaking Through in Prayer

Dedication

This book is dedicated to my wife, Nori, whose single greatest desire is that God fulfil His perfect will in me; and to the Holy Spirit, who taught me how to pray, gave me the desire to pray and placed me 'in Christ'.

Acknowledgements

My mother-in-law, Sally Floyd, who through faith and patience greatly contributed to the editorial process.

Breaking Through in Prayer

DAN CHESNEY

foreword by

PAUL YONGGI CHO

Marshall Pickering

Marshall Morgan and Scott
Marshall Pickering
3 Beggarwood Lane, Basingstoke, Hants RG23 7LP, UK

British Library CIP Data

Chesney, Dan
  Breaking through in prayer.
  1. Prayer
  I. Title
  248.3'2   BV210.2

ISBN: 0-551-01601-9

Text Set in Plantin by Brian Robinson Ltd, Buckingham, England.
Printed in Great Britain by Richard Clay Ltd, Bungay, Suffolk.

Contents

Foreword

A successful prayer life is to learn to know the heart of God and find out how intimate fellowship with Him can be in prayer. Prayer has changed the course of nations. It certainly has changed the course of our nation of Korea, and prayer will change the course of everyone who earnestly desires to have direction and answers for their personal life today.

The purpose of this book is to help the seeking Christian to realize there is a difference in praying from time to time to satisfy the conscience because one knows he should pray, and praying until one has broken through and touched God. If we have not learned to pray until our own barriers have come down we have not really learned to pray. Persisting, prevailing prayer is not easy but it will bring us great victory if we don't faint until we have prayed through. Everything that God made grows, and growth and development are important for every believer too. The greatest growth for the believer comes through prayer and the word, learning when to worship, when to listen, when to receive from Him, when to make our requests known and when to obey!

If you don't know whether you have touched God in your prayer time and received an assurance your requests you placed before Him have been heard, then you probably have not broken through in prayer.

As you read this book you will want to close its pages and begin to meditate on the truths you have read, so do it and then go back and read more.

I trust you will experience the 'breaking through' or 'praying through' for your personal needs and then go on to pray for family, friends, business and crisis situations. Great is our God and greatly to be praised but we will never know it unless we learn to pray until we break through and touch God. I trust this book will bless you richly again and again!

Paul Yonggi Cho
Yoido Full Gospel Church
Seoul, Korea

Introduction

There is a call to prayer from Heaven going out to the body of Christ worldwide. It is being orchestrated by none other than the Holy Spirit. Hearts are being stirred, churches are awakening and the intercession of the saints is being heard once again. All over the world prayer partners are forming into strategic armed forces who, under the Lordship of Jesus Christ their Commander-in-Chief, are storming the gates of Hell and taking back the land and its captives.

We are living in a time of unprecedented upheavals both in the natural and spiritual realms. Battles are being fought for the souls of man on earth and in the unseen heavenlies. And we have a part in determining the outcome of the war!

This is why the urgent call for prayer has gone forth. 'To loose the bonds of wickedness, to undo the heavy burdens, to let the oppressed go free, and that YOU break every yoke?' (Isa. 58:6 NKJV). The Lord is asking us a question. Will we break every yoke? We can if we know HOW to pray.

There are many who know they should pray, want to pray, and even spend time in prayer but they have never BROKEN THROUGH into ANSWERED prayer—that place where they are face to face with God and their soul has been touched with the power of Heaven.

Part One of this book is designed to help you BREAK THROUGH in prayer by understanding who you are in Christ Jesus. Once you have experienced being one with Christ your prayer life will know no boundaries. We will see that through the word, faith, the Holy Spirit and love we can enter into that understanding and abide there constantly. Meditate over and over on these chapters, asking the Holy Spirit to make this your foundation for prayer.

From there we will go on to discuss many of the more practical aspects of private prayer such as what to do with your body, how to develop a desire to pray and how to find time to pray daily. Part Two will help open your eyes to some of the unseen hinderances to prayer and give you the keys to conquer them.

I believe the Holy Spirit will use this book to give you that BREAK THROUGH in prayer and with God that you have been looking for!

PART I

Prayer
Our Pathway To Living
In Union With Christ

Chapter 1

What is Prayer

Are you hungry for God? Do you feel as though your thirst cannot be quenched except by the 'Living Springs'? Within man there is a destiny-consciousness created by God where deep calls unto deep, where the cry is sent up for 'the prize of the high calling of God in Christ'. Prayer, ever-expanding, ever-ascending, ever-reaching into the throne-room of God is that road which God uses to fulfill His destiny in us.

Highway To Heaven

My journey began the day the Lord spoke to me in prayer and said, 'I have set you on the road to the throne-room of God'. Since then I have learned that the road to God's throne-room is prayer, a glorious highway constructed solely for man to reach our Heavenly Father. It is a highway much like Moses, Aaron, Nadab, Abihu and the seventy elders each saw in a vision on Mount Sinai. 'And they saw the God of Israel; under His feet there seemed to be a pavement of brilliant sapphire stones, as clear as the heavens' (Ex 24:10 TLB). Our prayers are those stones, the building blocks of our relationship with God.

Furthermore, just as the pavement was transparent so that no one could see it except the ones who went up the mountain to be with God, so our prayers are unseen and unheard by man. We are instructed by Christ to 'go into your room, close the door and pray to your Father, who is unseen. Then your Father, who sees what is done in secret, will reward you' (Mt. 6:6 NIV). Yes, our prayers may be as unseen as that pavement, but when we emerge from our prayer closets, our Father who sees what is done in secret, rewards us by filling us with the life and power of the Holy Spirit, so that we shine, even as that pavement brilliantly sparkled, with the presence God. Is it any wonder Moses came down from Mount Sinai with his face radiating with the glory of heaven! Our prayers with God may be unseen, but when we come down from the mountain, they are visible because we have the answer in our hands.

Prayer is reciprocal. It is our heart responding to the heart of God. Moses and his leaders climbed up the mountain to their place of prayer in response to God's desire for fellowship with man, for the Lord said, 'Come up unto the Lord . . .' (Ex.24:1 KJV). Moses' obedience shows his willingness to fellowship with God. Prayer is man coming up to God and God coming down to man. Prayer, in response to God's desire and word, brings unity between God and man. That is the essence of prayer. Prayer is our union with God in action.

Praying is not just sending words from earth to heaven, but rather it is a transportation platform where *we* 'are constantly being transfigured into His very own image in ever increasing splendour and from one degree of glory to another; (for this comes) from the Lord (Who is) the Spirit' (2 Cor.3:18 AMP). Prayer is God's way of getting *us* to His throne-room and developing in us His own nature and likeness. It is getting God into the situation. We ascend into His presence and become more and more like Christ in likeness, in character, in essence and in understanding. It is what we are in Christ that causes our prayers to be what they are on earth. The word says, 'Let *us* (not just our words) therefore come boldly unto the throne of grace that *we* may obtain mercy, and find grace to help in time of need' (Heb. 4:16 KJV).

Prayer is a Relationship with God

Prayer is the development and formation of a relationship. It is getting to know God so well that you know

WHAT to pray, WHEN to pray and HOW to pray. It is not asking God to do something independent from us, but rather in conjunction with us. We are joint heirs with Christ, sharing a legal participation in Christ's inheritance. Part of the inheritance the Father gave His Son was the name of JESUS. Jesus has now given us the right to use His name because we are members of His family. Thus when the Father hears that name in prayer, it is just as if His Son is praying. This is why Jesus said unto His disciples, 'Then you will present your petitions over my signature! And I won't need to ask the Father to grant you these requests' (John 16:26 TLB). Through the new birth we are now part of a *divine* partnership, realized through prayer, the indispensable channel of communication.

As we build this highway up to heaven, the Father sends back His instructions, directions, answers and guidance so that we can follow through with 'Thy will be done on earth as it is in heaven' (Mt.6:10 KJV).

When scanning the past ages, one can see this God-ordained method called prayer shaping and reshaping history. For the Lord said to Isaiah, 'Ask Me of things to come concerning my sons, and concerning the work of My hands command ye Me' (Is. 45:11 KJV). These words are a command from Almighty God, challenging us to pick up the torch that was so effective in turning history towards salvation. Was it not prayer that parted the Red Sea, stopped the sun and moon in orbit, delivered Lot and his children from destruction, diverted the whole nation of Israel from God's wrath, built and rebuilt Solomon's temple, birthed the New Testament Church and thus turned the world upside down? On and on we see all of heaven waiting to hear 'the effectual fervent prayer of righteous man . . .' for it has 'availed much'. As it was for them so it is for us; all of heaven awaits our call: 'Call upon Me and I will answer thee and show thee great and mighty things which thou knowst not' (Jer. 33:3).

Let your eyes be opened as Elisha's servant's were, so you may know 'they that be with us are more than they that be with them' (2 Kings 6:16 KJV). Heaven is the place where 'all those ministering spirits are sent to serve those who will inherit salvation' (Heb. 1:14 NIV). Only 'in seeing' will we not fear. Elisha was a man of prayer and therefore 'saw' the heavenly host. His servant was not and therefore feared. It was Elisha's *prayer* that brought those angels down from heaven to earth, and Jesus has given us the authority to pray this same kind of prayer when He taught us to say, 'but deliver us from evil'. The Father is waiting to answer, but unless we pray that prayer, He is unable.

As I have sat at the feet of Jesus like Mary, having the Holy Spirit 'who leads us into all truth' teach me how to pray, I have seen this highway as the jewel of God's heart, the key to knowing Him. Be encouraged and know you can enter into the throne-room of the One 'whose ears are always open to His saints'.

It was my custom to arise each morning at 4:30 for prayer and reading of His word, but one one particular morning I was very tired. As the alarm went off, I reached over and silenced it, saying to myself, 'I'll get up in just a few minutes'. Soon I was drifting off into the world of sleep, but just before reaching to edge of unconsciousness, I heard the Holy Spirit speak to me in an audible voice, saying, 'Jesus is waiting for you'. It was a voice of majesty and beauty. It was full of love yet firm. I flung off the blankets and ran into the other room to fall upon my knees in prayer. My friend, Jesus is waiting for you, too. Will you not rise out of your sleep and fellowship with Him?

Chapter 2

The Purpose of Prayer

The Prophet Joel prophesied, 'And it shall come to pass in the last days, says God, that I will pour out of My Spirit on all flesh. Your young men shall see visions, your old men shall dream dreams . . .' (Acts 2:17 NKJV). Within those visions and dreams is *your* destiny in the Kingdom of our Christ, and prayer is the key to breaking through and placing them back into the hands of the architect, Almighty God.

'For he looked for a city which hath foundations whose builder and maker is God.'

(Heb. 11:10 KJV)

Praying God's Will

The disciples came to Jesus one day and asked Him, 'Lord, teach us to pray' (Luke 11:1 KJV) and Jesus answered them with 'When ye pray, say . . ., Thy Kingdom come. Thy will be done in earth, as it is in heaven' (Mt. 6:10 KJV). These divinely breathed words in response to the questioning disciples revealed to them and to us the whole purpose and sum total of all prayer: transferring God's Kingdom from heaven to earth. This is the heart of the matter; prayer is the answer by which God can and will establish his Kingdom, His will, His nature, His life, His character and His solutions in man for every situation. There can be no greater purpose to pray than to see 'the earth . . . filled with the knowledge of the glory of the

Lord, as the waters cover the sea' (Hab. 2:14 KJV).

When God established the earth and created man, it was heaven on earth, the will of God was being done as Adam and Eve walked with God. Perfect harmony existed and would exist as long as they communicated with the Father, 'praying without ceasing'. All was only good and divine as the Kingdom of God was being established, but when they failed to call upon God in prayer, they sinned, with evil, sadness and separation following. If only Adam and Eve had consulted, prayed, turned to God when the devil tempted them, rather than relying upon their own reasoning and emotional abilities. God would have answered them, but they failed to avail themselves of that privilege called prayer. Man's first cause for sin was prayerlessness, and it is still the root of all of man's failures. Adam's *prayerlessness* led to separation, and separation leads to further prayerlessness. Oh! if only Adam had called upon God, surely He would have 'showed him great and mighty things', their enemy vanquished, the trial ended and peace reigning once again. Adam did not pray, 'Thy will be done in earth, as it is in heaven' and so another kingdom established its rulership on the foundation of disobedience.

When God sent His Son to earth, did He not say, 'The Kingdom of God is among you'? The Father's will never changes, His heart's desire was and is to see man lifted from the 'kingdom of darkness and translated into the Kingdom of His dear Son' (Col. 1:13).

Jesus was heaven on earth, He was 'Thy Kingdom come; Thy will be done in earth as it is in heaven'. This God-man, Jesus the Saviour, came because man prayed, for from the fall of man up to His appearing, the saints and prophets alike were faithfully requesting in an endless stream of prayer the Kingdom of God to come. Abraham, Moses, David, Solomon, Isaiah, Jeremiah, Ezekiel, one after another formed a relay of prayer, until finally we read of Anna the prophetess, a woman who 'served God with fastings and prayer'. Night and day she was looking for the redemption in Israel. Day and night this woman prayed, 'Thy Kingdom come'. Were these prayers to no avail? No, for Anna saw the Messiah, the answer to her prayer and all the prayers that went before her.

Our Part

And now, what are our instructions for prayer? They are the same; the final word left to us by the Revelation of John is, 'and the Spirit and the bride say, Come' (Rev. 22:17 KJV). Today, with the advent of the Holy Spirit indwelling the believer, how much more efficacious our prayers can be '. . . The Spirit helps us in our weakness. We do not know what we ought to pray, but the Spirit himself intercedes for the saints in accordance with God's will' (Rom. 8:26–27 NIV). The Holy Spirit and man can be in agreement that God's will be done 'in earth as it is in heaven'.

Let us arise in faith and recognize that prayer is what puts the Son of God in possession of His Kingdom on earth. Jesus said, 'And I will give unto thee the keys of the Kingdom of heaven: and whatsoever thou shalt bind on earth shall be bound in heaven: and whatsoever thou shalt loose on earth shall be loosed in heaven' (Mt. 16:19 KJV). We who walk this earth have keys to a Kingdom in heaven. And one of those keys loosening this earth to receive the Kingdom of heaven is prayer. Jesus spoke of prayer when He said, 'Whatsoever YOU bind, Whatsoever YOU loosen'. Binding the kingdom of darkness and loosening the Kingdom of heaven is an activity of prayer. Jesus is not saying He will do the binding and loosening – no, He is saying *we* will do it. *Then* the Father will answer. 'Whatsoever ye shall ask the Father in My name, He will give it you' (John 16:23 KJV).

E.M. Bounds said, 'Prayer is one prime, eternal condition by which the Father is pledged to put the Son in Possession of the world'. How can we complain of the unrighteousness in government, in education, in our society when we realize that righteousness only reigns as we pray the 'effectual fervent prayer'. *We* determine the influence of light or darkness, of Christ or Satan; of God's Kingdom or the devil's rulership. Isaiah tells us, 'When the enemy shall come in like a flood, the Spirit of the Lord shall lift up a standard against him or shall put him to flight' (Is. 59:19 KJV).

How? Through the Church! We are the standard the Spirit lifts up. Jesus confirmed this when he said, '. . . I will build my church and the gates of hell shall not prevail against it' (Mt. 16:18 KJV), 'it' meaning the Church, you and me. We are the ones who 'resist the devil and he will flee'; we are the ones who take 'the sword of the Spirit . . .' 'and praying always with all prayer and supplication in the Spirit . . .' we are the ones instructed to 'stand'. As awesome a responsibility as it may seem, God has delegated to His Church the authority and duty of setting the boundaries of God's Kingdom on earth, which also means that by prayer-lessness, we allow hell to enlarge its borders on earth.

It was no light thing when Jesus said to His disciples, 'Watch and pray, that ye enter not into temptation'. If Adam had watched and prayed, just imagine the glory and progress of Christ's Kingdom on earth today; but through his sin of prayerlessness, he set the plan of God back nearly 7,000 years. All temptation is designed to stop man from communing with God, to break that fellowship, to separate the Kingdom of heaven from earth; thus, all prayer, true prayer is a safeguard against temptation. The only remedy for prayerlessness is prayer.

Ever since Adam's fall, man has been struggling to regain what was lost. History is filled with man's ingenious ideas and ways of recreating 'paradise lost'; religiousity, technology, medical panaceas, science, shangri-la's, drugs, knowledge. Man pursues one utopia after another. And in the background of man's activity we hear the voice of the Father saying, 'Ask, and it shall be given'. Prayer is man's carte blanche with God. Whatsoever we ask He shall give. What more could God promise us than His Kingdom, His Son, His All, in response to our prayers. Did not the Lord appear to Solomon in I Kings 3:5 and 'told him to ask for anything he wanted, and it would be given to him' (LB). The historical accounts of successful prayer recorded in the Bible reveal to us this one abiding principle of 'Thy will be done in earth as it is in heaven'. This principle is indeed the composition and heartbeat of requests of praying saints. Over and over this message is reiterated to us so that 'we (can) have such confidence in Him that we are certain that

He hears every request made in accord with His own PLAN. And since we KNOW He invariably gives His attention to our prayers, whatever they are about, we can be quite sure that our prayers will be answered' (1 John 5:14–15 JBP).

Now that we know what prayer is – a relationship with God, and why we are to pray – to establish God's kingdom on earth – we can begin to look at what makes prayer work – our union with Christ.

Chapter 3

The Prayer of Fellowship

These words spake Jesus, and lifted up
His eyes to heaven, and said, Father . . .
I pray for them . . . That they may be one;
as Thou, Father, art in me, and I in thee,
that they also may be one in us: that the
world may believe that Thou hast sent me.

(John 17:1,9,21 KJV)

The Hidden Jewel of Prayer

There is a hidden jewel of prayer that many have not found, or have forgotten, called fellowship. It is this facet of the diamond that, if turned just so, catches the brightness of the light and reveals the veiled beauty. In the prayer of fellowship, a child of God actually experiences the presence and person of Almighty God. Here is where you and the Father meet, exchanging the intimate secrets of your hearts. It is the holy ground upon which you hear the voice of the Father speaking, singing to your soul, a place of rest and tranquility, of still waters and green pastures. It is like discovering a natural bird habitat hidden away from man and civilization, where there is no fear of danger or distress, where only harmony and peace abide. Nothing has been disturbed, there have been no alterations or changes, and it remains pure like the garden of Eden; it is God only.

Fellowship is found in that, often unread, book of the Bible, the Song of Solomon. Here you can read the words of the bride and the bridegroom, of Christ and His Church in the prayer closet of close fellowship where they see only each other through eyes of love. 'Let him kiss me with the kisses of his mouth,' 'Draw me, we will run after thee: The King hath brought me into his chambers.' It is only in this chamber that love is shared in trust, 'Beloved, thou art fair, my love'. This is the nearness we hear when our Saviour calls, 'Rise up my love, my fair one, and come away' (S. of S. 1:2,4,15; 2:10 KJV). Surely this is the place where David was when he said, 'In thy presence is the fulness of joy, at thy right hand are pleasures evermore' (Ps. 16:11 KJV).

This is the place of God only, no others. Not self, not angels, not demons, but only God are you experiencing. It is 'the secret place of the most high' (Ps. 91:1 KJV), the cleft of the rock where Moses sat and beheld the back of God, the leaning of John, the Beloved, on the Lord's breast.

Our Union with Christ

Here you will discover the length, breadth, depth and height of God, and here you will see *your* place *in* Christ. As you learn to draw ever nearer in fellowship with the Father, an undeniable process begins to take place which is called, 'being changed into the SAME image of His dear Son . . .' (2 Cor. 3:18 AMP). Here, as we enter into the holy of holies, it is the Father's good pleasure to give us a revelation of our oneness with Christ, to unveil to us our union and likeness with His Son, through the new birth. You begin to decrease and Christ begins to increase.

The Hebrew word for 'wait' in Isaiah 40:31 is *'qaveh'* (kawveh) which means 'to twist or bind together'. Therefore, as we are waiting (fellowshipping) upon the Lord, our lives are being twisted and bound up together. Christ is literally being melded into our being. The nature, abilities, characteristics and substances of Christ becomes intertwined with our recreated human spirit. Paul writes, 'And put on the new nature (the regenerate self) created in God's image, (Godlike) in true righteousness and holiness' (Eph. 4:24 AMP). Our nature now consists of Christ's righteousness and holiness. This reborn spirit of ours is made up of the same substance as Christ and has the ability to grow up into 'the measure of the stature of the fulness of Christ' (Eph. 4:13 KJV). Isaiah prophesied this day when he said 'This is the heritage of the servants of the Lord, and their righteousness is of me, saith the Lord' (Is. 54:17 KJV). Could God have given us His nature if we had not been created in His image and likeness? No! Two different natures cannot form a union. Paul tells us, 'What common interest can there be between goodness and evil? How can light and darkness share life together? How can there be harmony between Christ and the devil? What business can a believer have with an unbeliever?' (2 Cor. 6:14–15 JBP). NONE, and that is why God has given us a new nature, a rebirth, so a union of fellowship *can* be established. Am I saying that we are God or can become God? No, no more than a son can become his father. He is forever God and we are forever His sons, but nonetheless we share His nature, His likeness, the stamp of His image even as a son his father's.

We are partakers of His divine nature because our recreated spirit now has an affinity for His Spirit. As the branch is to the vine, as the body is to the head, as Eve was to Adam, all of the same substance, of like nature, so are we to Christ. He has given us that nature, so now, His Spirit and life can flow into us. All that Christ is now becomes our life, Christ becomes the new you so that you can herald, 'Not I, but Christ'. What Christ is, is now poured into you. John writes, 'For as He is, so are we in this world' (1 John 5:17 KJV). Why? Because Christ is in us and we are in Him. This is the great love story of the Bible, of God reaching to man and drawing him into His bosom, a new creation created in His image. God gave us His nature so that we could be like Him. This is the grace Paul sang out by saying, 'I am what I am by the grace of God' (1 Cor. 15:10 KJV).

After Paul's Damascus road experience, he went to Arabia, determined to know his new-found love. There, like Moses, in quiet solitude, he rises from his knees with light in his eyes and a flaming love in his heart proclaiming, 'But he that is joined unto the Lord is one spirit' (2 Cor. 6:16 KJV). Through fellowship, the Father revealed to Paul just how far His divine grace can reach – God uniting Himself to man.

Can the finite mind grasp the wisdom of the infinite, that He has made us His extended family? No, but because of our union, 'Incredible as it may sound, we who are spiritual have the very thoughts of Christ!' (1 Cor. 2:16 JBP). In the Old Testament, God's thoughts were higher than man's thoughts and His ways were higher than man's ways but now, with the advent of Christ's work on Calvary, He has said, 'I will put my laws into their minds and write them in their hearts . . .' (Heb. 8:10 KJV)

In every letter and with every breath, Paul and the other New Testament writers breathed out with ringing triumph this masterful love-gift of our heavenly Father – we are bone of his bone and flesh of His flesh, 'And we are all members of that body; we are His flesh and blood!' (Eph. 5:30 JBP). The true Church of Jesus Christ is *His* body, Ephesians 1:22–23 says, 'For the Church is His body, and in that body lives fully the one who fills the whole wide universe'.

What a revelation Paul received when he discovered God's purpose and destiny for him, for Christ to be revealed in him. We with our varied personalities make up this body of Christ, the Church, through which the Father by the Holy Spirit is revealing the many-sided glory of Christ. Just as some develop their muscles, so, in the realm of the Spirit, the strength of Christ is revealed. Some become masters with their hands, showing the ministry of Christ; others show great promise of intellect, representing the wisdom of Christ. We are all members of His body, forming one person, Christ!

It is clear that Christ is the head of the Church, but it is also clear that the work of the Holy Spirit is to enable the body to chorus out, 'Not I, but Christ'. Therefore, if we have died, if we have decreased, if the body has put off the old man, then who is the new man who has increased, who has resurrected – the Christ in us. By faith Christ and His body became one identity. Have you ever known a person who called his body by one name and his head by another? NO, they are one, and so are we one in Christ.

Like Adam and Eve, we through the new birth are once

again linked to the second Adam and made into His image anew. We are in union with His nature. Christ the head and we His body, organically linked, now becoming 'partakers of His divine nature' or 'God's essential nature' (2 Peter 1:3 KJV & JBP).

Here at His feet we are 'constantly being transfigured into His own image in ever increasing splendour and from one degree of glory to another' (2 Cor. 3:18 AMP). No wonder the Psalmist exclaims, 'He has crowned us with glory and honour' (Ps. 8:5 KJV). What glory is endowed upon man when he is divinely birthed by the heavenly Father, thereby receiving His very own genetic make-up. 1 John 3:9 tells us that we have received 'His principle of life, the divine sperm' (AMP). We bear the DNA of our heavenly Father even as we do our earthly parents. We have now become 'Part of the permanent' (1 John 2:17 JBP). We have found our roots, our genealogy along with John who wrote, 'Ye are of God'. The question is settled, 'In Christ (He is) we are a new creature: old things are passed away; behold, all things are become new' (2 Cor. 5:17 KJV).

Prayer – A Divine Romance

Fellowship is nothing less than a divine romance. He woos us, courts us and then marries us, the two becoming one. Here is where Daniel heard those words, 'O Daniel, a man greatly beloved . . .' (Dan. 10:11 KJV). Here in the prayer of fellowship you become lost in Him, filled with Him, embraced by Him and He whispers to your heart, 'I in you and you in me' (John 14:20 KJV). Here is where 'perfect love casts out fear' (1 John 4:18 NKJV). John could not contain himself from sharing this relationship, so he writes, 'That ye also may have fellowship with us: and truly our fellowship is with the Father, and with His Son Jesus Christ' (1 John 1:3 KJV).

The Father yearns and longs for, and has even ordained this relationship with us. His will for every believer is that we abide in Christ, to be one and in union with Christ. Paul, when receiving this revelation could no longer see himself independent of Christ and, therefore, writes, 'for me to live is Christ' (Phil. 1:21 KJV). Christ and Paul had been eternally joined in holy union. Is it any wonder when Paul came from his *prayer closet* he became a fearless defender of the faith. The cause of Christ became his cause, the Gospel of Christ became his Gospel, the death, resurrection and glorification of Christ became his death, resurrection and glorification. To think that man can share and identify with Christ so as to say, 'Remember that Jesus Christ of the seed of David was raised from the dead, according to my gospel' (2 Tim. 2:8 KJV).

With such an identify, Paul could go anywhere, be with anybody and still His Lord was with him, enabling, strengthening, assuring, loving, comforting and empowering. Like Enoch, Noah, Abraham, and many others, he not only had died, been resurrected and ascended with Christ, but also walked with Christ. This is fellowship, walking so near and experiencing with Christ such intimacy that nothing less than a union can result. Such closeness can only respond, 'I am my beloved's and He is mine' (S. of S. 2:16).

Can you not hear the Lord calling, 'Draw nigh unto me and I will draw nigh unto you' (James 4:8 KJV)? He has given us wings that we may use them to draw close; 'for they that wait upon the Lord shall renew their strength, they shall mount up with wings as eagles' (Is. 40:31 KJV); up, up and into His realm these wings take us, for He has said, '. . . I bare you on eagle's wings, and brought you unto myself' (Ex. 19:4 KJV). *There*, this is the purpose of the wings, to ascend unto Him!

What glory He has planned for those who will desire one thing from the Lord and seek after it, and that is, 'I shall be satisfied, when I awake with His likeness' (Ps. 17:15 KJV). These people will experience on earth what others will only experience in heaven. Rees Howell describes this by saying:

'So nigh, so very nigh to God, I cannot nearer be; for in the person of the Son, I am as near as He'.

The well-spring of this relationship is Christ in us, giving us continuous, intimte fellowship. This is what Jesus meant when He said, 'I am the vine, you are the branches' (John 15:5 NKJV). Christ gives us life and strength, like the rain

27

that falls from heaven and it is then drawn up by the roots of our spirits, living plants. His thoughts become our thoughts, His (*zoe*) life our (*zoe*) life, His nearness to the Father our nearness now. It is only through the PRAYER of fellowship that what has taken place in our spirit man at the new birth now finds expression and becomes a living reality. Do not wait until you get to heaven, but on your knees find that 'the Kingdom of heaven is at hand' (Mt. 4:17).

You ask the question, can such a relationship be mine? The answer is YES, 'for all the promises of God in him are yea, and in him Amen . . .' (2 Cor. 1:20 KJV). The promises can only be ours because we are 'in Him'. This fellowship is the jewel that every overcoming saint coveted and held precious to his heart. In the depths of the souls of those men and women arose the cry, 'Abba, Father' (Rom. 8:15). There is no greater privilege than experiencing this union with the Son of God, of growing and allowing the divine life of Christ to flow and permeate our consciousness.

Becoming Family

What 'joy unspeakable and full of glory' that the Son of God became the Son of man, so we, the sons of man could become the sons of God. Christ 'has raised us up and made us to sit together with Him in heavenly places' (Eph. 2:6 KJV). We are heirs of God, joint heirs with Christ; we are family. Therefore, the offer has been extended to us to 'come up hither' (Rev. 4:1 KJV) right into His throne-room. His presence, 'for our life is hid with Christ in God' (Col. 3:2 KJV).

As family, we are an extension of the Godhead, just as children are to their earthly family. The Father calls us sons and daughters, Jesus calls us His brethren (Heb. 2:12 KJV). Why? Because once being 'baptized into Christ (we) have put on the family likeness of Christ' (Gal. 3:27 JBP). What a revelation of His love that we should be called the 'children of God,' and that is not just what we are called, but what we *are*. Listen to the excitement of John as he further writes, 'We only know that, if reality were to *break through*, we should reflect his likeness, for we should see him as he really is!' (1 John 3:1 JBP). Yes, we shall be like Him when we see him at the second coming, but even now, through fellowship, we can 'see' Him, and as we see Him, we do realize our family likeness to Him. What joy this brings to the ones whose earthly family has been shattered, for in Christ there are no illegitimate children. We have been legally birthed by the Father. There are no battered children, for like a mother hen, He gathers us under His feathers and protects us. He is a Father to the fatherless. He is El-Shaddai, the breasty-one to the hungry and thirsty. He is the instructor to the wayward son, the Father to the prodigal, the healer to the brokenhearted. His is a family of love and unity, of peace and caring.

We must not be afraid of this closeness, this intimacy, this union, for it is the result of our salvation. Listen to Moses as he dared to prophesy, 'The Lord thy God will raise up unto thee a prophet from the midst of thee, of thy brethren, like unto *me* . . .' (Deut. 18:15 KJV). '*Like unto me*' – it took a divinely inspired faith for Moses to confess that, and yet, he was able to leave a legacy behind him giving us a glimpse into his prayer life.

The prayer of fellowship is a foretaste of our life to be in heaven, a glimpse of the unsearchable gift, the cry of the human heart panting after God. Through fellowship you can come to know God and who you are in Him. It is this discovery that makes all prayer efficacious. When Moses received a new revelation of God in the cleft of the rock, he later used that knowledge to intercede for the Israelites, which brought great results. Thus also did all the saints, for as they spent time in fellowship, they came to know Him, making them capable of praying aright. They were enabled to 'walk in the Light as he is in the Light' and be imitators of 'Christ' because of this closeness (1 John 1:7).

God – The Main Ingredient

So many Christians miss the joy of prayer because they have left out the main ingredient – God. We have perhaps concentrated too much on the asking or speaking, the crying or fomulas, and this in turn has bred boredom. Let all our prayers burst forth out of fellowship with the Father because then they are filled with the life and power of Christ. No longer is it just your words, but it is your life in union with Christ that is being offered up. The Father will not deny His Son, and, as we approach Him in Christ, He will not deny us either.

I remember the day when I broke through, after long days, yes, even years in prayer, the revelation broke like lightning. It struck my heart like an explosion, and my spirit was aflame with my union with Christ. In a moment of time the room and I seemed full of light. He had raised me up and made me sit together in heavenly places in Christ.

So filled was I with the revelation of Christ that I saw myself reigning with Him in dominion, authority, power and victory. I was one with the Conqueror. His love joined me to Him.

There was no thought of self, but only Him. From death to faith, from self to Christ, from seeking to rest. Oh, how blessed are those who hunger and thirst after righteousness for they shall be filled. Now I am possessed of my lover only. I no longer have to fear, for He is the keeper of His new domain, me. I am kept in the union with my Saviour.

The time I've spent in prayer with Thee
has been the secret and hidden key.
Spirit to spirit, heart to heart,
you've compelled me on.
With light you've opened my darkened mind,
transforming me upward into Your kind.
You've drawn so near my soul has sung,
in union, in union! The prize I've won!

D.C.

Chapter 4

Our Foundation for Prayer The Abrahamic Covenant

Prayer is what opens the door for God to involve Himself with and in the person praying and in that person's request. It is petitioning God, and all that He is, to be poured into mankind's spirit, soul, body and circumstances, thus making life on earth a heavenly experience.

The prayer life of Jesus exemplified, 'Thy will be done on earth as it is in heaven' (Mt. 6:10 KJV), because it was God the Father expressing Himself in Christ. The Lord's prayer life permitted the Father full expression towards mankind, which explains such results in His ministry.

As we now pray, having a relationship of being in union with Christ, it is Christ in us, expressing Himself, even as it was the Father in Christ when he walked the earth. Mark 16:20 says, 'They went forth and preached everywhere, the Lord working in them . . .'. Answered prayer was simply Christ visible on earth through the Apostles. The Pharisees, when observing the ministry and boldness of the Apostles, commented, 'That they (the Apostles) had been with Jesus' (Acts 4:13 KJV). This is the secret, they had been with Jesus in prayer, prayer of such close fellowship that they had been joined to Christ.

May our eyes be open to see that our union with Christ, our being 'in Christ' is the one and all-inclusive assurance that our prayers will be answered. Jesus said, 'Father, I thank thee that thou hast heard me . . . and I know that thou hearest me always . . .' (John 11:41–42 KJV). This

31

shows the unquestionable willingness of the Father to always answer Jesus, and, since we have now been engrafted into Him by faith, then the Father is equally willing to answer us.

The Purpose of Man

God created man for fellowship, for a relationship, for a family. His desire is to work *with* us, not independent of us. This is why He has called us co-labourers, joint heirs, ambassadors, sons of God, His body; all these require an active, vital relationship. He will not work in spite of or contrary to us. He desires partnership. It is an offence for God to work independent of man and vice versa. This can best be seen in the marriage relationship. If a spouse were to operate independently of or irrespective of the other spouse, then a breach would develop to break the bond of unity. God has made the husband and wife 'heirs together of the grace of life' (1 Peter 3:7 KJV) and, the two shall become one flesh. Self-reliance becomes offensive. In a relationship, two are to be one.

When Adam acted independently of God's word, he broke the bond and created a breach in their relationship. God had said to him, 'for in the day that thou eatest thereof (the fruit of the tree of the knowledge of good and evil) thou shalt surely die' (Gen. 2:17 KJV). And he did, he died spiritually. This shows us the power of the word, for as long as Adam kept God's word, or what we might even call a verbal contract, he was blessed. But the moment he disobeyed, the link between God and man was severed; thus man put himself outside of God's jurisdiction to bless him as He desired. God's ability to keep man is partially limited to man's keeping God's word, for it is faith in God's word that unites man to God.

Now, some may say, if it is up to man to keep God's Word, we will fail. Yes, and that was proven by the Law; but His grace has gone beyond the mere keeping of the law; He has given us the Holy Spirit. In Christians the Holy Spirit is working in us both to *will* and to *do* for His good pleasure. He puts the desire to obey and choose God's will within us. And even when we are separated from God, the Spirit will woo us, reveal to us, speak to us, and influence us to choose Christ.

God's heart was still the same, His Father's love was still affectionate towards man, but man had gone astray, broken the fellowship, shattered the relationship – and man without the word was like a boat drifting out to sea. How could the two be reconciled? How could communion be re-established, how could man, who was in darkness, pray to God who is the Light? What grounds does man have to come into the Father's presence now? As long as Adam had kept God's word, the door was open, for it was the word that *gave* Adam the right and privilege to commune with God. But Adam had rejected that word, he had destroyed the very foundation or promise upon which his right of access was founded.

It is here that the marvellous grace of God is seen. Man cannot reconcile himself to God, and neither can he ascend into heaven to approach the throne of grace, for he is earth bound, sin stained and imprisoned by Satan. How can he pray or cry for mercy when he has no bill of rights, the Word of God, to cry upon? He had thrown them away in the garden. The need for God's word again is clear, for it is in the word that all prayers, all communion and all fellowship are established. And so, 'God sent His word and delivered them from their destruction' (Ps. 107:20 KJV). Yes, 'while we were yet sinners, Christ (the Word) died for us (Rom. 5:8 KJV).

If God was ever to save man, and if man was ever to have access to God again, God needed His word in the earth once more. So the romance continued, God's infinite love searching for a man that would accept and keep His word.

God found such men as Abel, Enoch and Noah who responded to His word, and as time went on, God was able to build and reconstruct that shattered relationship with man. This progressed until the time of Abraham. It is here that God begins, with this man, to establish a document of grace of such magnitude that its provision would encompass the needs of all mankind. This is known as the Abrahamic Covenant.

The Abrahamic Covenant

This covenant was designed so God could join Himself to man once again, save him from his sins, and restore him back into the image of God as He had created Adam. It began when God appeared unto Abraham and said, '. . . Get thee out of thy country, and from thy kindred, and from thy father's house, unto a land that I will show thee: And I will make of thee a great nation, and I will bless thee, and make thy name great; and thou shalt be a blessing; And I will bless them that bless thee, and curse him that curseth thee; and in thee shall all families of the earth be blessed' (Gen. 12:1–3 KJV). This was God giving His word or covenant to Abraham, the covenant that would give man the right to pray, and that would draw him back into union with Jesus Christ.

For the next ten chapters of Genesis, God continued to elaborate on this covenant, giving Abraham more and more promises. Abraham could reject the covenant of blessings, but if he did, there could be no fulfillment of God's promises, just as we can reject the cup of blessing, limiting God's access into the lives of mankind on earth. The covenant was designed by God and initiated by God, but implied in every promise, contract or covenant is the acceptance of it by the recipients. This acceptance of God's promises is faith. Therefore, the way Abraham was to receive the promises of the covenant was by faith in God.

Genesis 15:6 tells us that Abraham, 'believed in the Lord; and He (God) counted it to him for righteousness'. Now that Abraham believed God's word, or covenant, this put him in right-standing with the Father which accomplished two things, allowing him to receive the blessings provided in the Covenant and enabling him to enter God's presence.

His prayers now had direction; he knew what he could pray for, and he knew that God would answer because they had a covenant. God and man were once again united, they were a team working together. God had access back into the earth, and man had access back into heaven.

As we read the story of Abraham, we now can see God working in him. Everywhere he went blessings followed;

rulers and common people alike sensed the divine favour that radiated from him. People therefore, wanted either to befriend him or make a covenant with him. God was once again revealing Himself through man. Abraham could have said, even as Paul did, 'I am crucified with Christ, nevertheless I live, yet not I, but Christ liveth in me . . .' (Gal. 2:20 KJV). God and man were linked up, united as family by His marvellous proposal of love called the covenant. Now, with this covenant in the earth, man, the prodigal, could find his way back by simply hearing and believing, even as Abraham did. We can see why such a covenant was so sacred and beyond value; it was the redemption of man's soul.

The word covenant means 'to cut', and in most of history whenever a covenant was to be formed between two people, families, tribes or natives, each person would cut themselves and then mingle their blood. Thus it was by the shedding of blood that a covenant came to be the most intimate, binding relationship between two individuals, and this is what God was offering to Abraham.

For Abraham to enter into this covenant with God was no light matter; it meant a complete committment of himself, even to the point of giving his life to God if the need arose. And this is what the word 'believe' means in Genesis 15:6, 'to give oneself wholly up', or to yield oneself completely to the will of Jehovah. God, on the other hand, was equally binding Himself to Abraham even to the point of giving *His* life. Thus the essence of the covenant was God's all for Abraham's all. God and Abraham were binding themselves to their word even if it meant death to make good the promise.

This covenant was ratified when God gave Abraham the rite of circumcision. Through the cutting of Abraham's flesh, blood was shed, and as a pledge of God's faithfulness, He told Abraham to take an animal as a substitute and slay it. In this way the blood covenant was established. They had cut the covenant and had now entered into a binding agreement of God's all for Abraham's all. Each took the responsibility for keeping his word.

As we behold God and then man, we can see that

Abraham obviously benefited to the greater extent in this covenant. God had promised only blessings, and Abraham had only to receive them by faith and obedience.

Therefore, as long as Abraham believed God's word, his prayer life was vital, for God had promised the giving of *His* life that He would keep His word. And so as Abraham put his faith in this covenant, he had a sure foundation for answered prayer. It was through this covenant that God could ask of Abraham and Abraham of God.

An example can be seen in Genesis 18 where God comes to Abraham and says, 'Shall I hide from Abraham that thing which I do; seeing that Abraham shall surely become a great and mighty nation, and all the nations of the earth shall be blesed in him?' (Gen. 18:17–18 KJV).

Judgment was about to fall upon the cities of Sodom and Gomorrah because of their sins, and evidently the wickedness was so severe and pervasive that in all of the two cities there was not one man who could pray the 'effectual and fervent prayer' for the righteous to be spared, let alone for the ungodly to be saved. Such was the corruption that the righteous could not even pray his way out of being judged along with the sinners. This is why God needed a covenant man, a man who could pray according to His word and believe that God would answer. Abraham's prayer, based on the blood covenant, was God's avenue of mercy into Lot's life. This is why God informed Abraham, because one of God's promises in the covenant was that 'all the nations of the earth would be blessed in him' (Gen. 18;18 KJV). Sodom and Gomorrah were a nation and could therefore be blessed. Abraham saw God's desire to save the cities and began to intercede. Here God and man were working as a team to save all who would be willing to be saved, but it could not be done without covenant prayer. Abraham's prayer was contracting God's heavenly construction company to come down and build His Kingdom. In Lot's case, it took heavy equipment to do it.

Through answers to prayer like these, God proved His covenant. As for Abraham, his trust grew. So convinced and trusting was he in this blood covenant, that when the

Lord asked him to sacrifice Isaac, there was no wavering on his part. Even though Abraham and Sarah had stood in faith for 25 years for Isaac, even though Isaac meant more to them than their own lives, and knowing that the promises of God could only be fulfilled through Isaac, yet they believed God's word. We see Abraham's heart in Hebrews 'accounting that God was able to raise him up, even from the dead'. Here is the power, authority and faith of this covenant, for Abraham believed it was impossible for God *not* to answer his prayer since it was birthed out of the covenant. Even if Isaac were sacrificed, God would still make His promises good, and since the promise was through Isaac, there was only one possibility, for Isaac to be raised from the dead!

Can you not see the smile of Abraham's face and confidence in his heart as he walked up Mount Moriah? It was the same for Elijah as he walked up Mount Carmel and for David as he walked towards Goliath. Their obedience to the covenant was drawing them into union with the Lord – a union that is more than rhetoric and theology, but rather a living, breathing, vital link between God and man. So close is this union that we can see this same scene reinacted as Jesus, the True Lamb, walked up Mount Calvary in obedience to the Father, to rid man of that one barrier that eclipsed our possible union with God – sin. Yes, Abraham's walk was a prophetic prelude to the steps of Jesus and the new covenant. As Abraham climbed up the mountain, he was climbing up into Christ. Beloved, do you not hear the glorified Christ calling you up into His Mount? 'He has raised us up and made us to sit in heavenly places in Christ Jesus' (Eph. 2:6).

Abraham's walk was one of intimate fellowship and security. El-Shaddai had never failed him, and now, in the hour of testing, the giving of his all, did he hesitate? No! Was there fear? No! He laid his only son on the altar, raised the knife . . . and his prayer was answered. The Angel of the Lord shouted, 'Abraham, Abraham . . . lay not thine hand upon the lad . . .' (Gen. 22: 11,12 KJV). God Himself provided a lamb and Isaac was saved.

Abraham's act of obedience solidified a priceless piece of

heavenly legislation. Thousands of years later Jesus Christ was born of the seed of Abraham, in spite of the ravages of captivity, war, and sin – nothing could stop the covenant from working; Christ was born!

This covenant had been ratified by three things, the oath, the promise, and the sacrifice. Genesis 22:16 says, '. . . By Myself have I sworn (this is the oath, a binding agreement from God Himself that He would keep His word) saith the Lord, for because thou hast done this thing, and hast not withheld thy son, thine only son: That in blessing I will bless thee . . .' (this is the promise) and then the shedding of blood by the animal sacrifice. Herein lies the confidence of Abraham.

Now all men who accepted this covenant could pray with the same assurance that Abraham did. God had given His oath, His promise, and pledged His Son's life to answer man's covenant prayers.

Moses, whose union with Christ was described as 'face to face' was able to deliver the Israelites because God remembered His covenant to Abraham, Isaac and Jacob. David was a man who 'gave himself unto prayer because God had spoken unto him saying, 'I have made a covenant with my chosen, I have sworn unto David my servant' (Ps. 89:3). No wonder David danced before the ark of the covenant! It was his assurance of answered prayer.

In Daniel 9 we get a glimpse into Daniel's secret of success. 'And I prayed unto the Lord my God, and made my confession, and said, O Lord, the great and dreadful God, keeping the *covenant* and mercy to them that love him, and them that keep His commandments' (Dan. 9:4). Daniel was asking for Christ to reign as Lord once again in Israel, but Daniel knew, as E.M. Bounds so beautifully put it, that, 'standing as the endowment of the enthroned Christ is the oath-bound covenant of the Father: "Ask of me, and I will give thee the heathen for thine inheritance, and the uttermost parts of the earth for thy possession"'. Daniel knew God was a covenant-keeping God, and so that was the grounds upon which he prayed.

Covenant prayers are more than just prayers based upon the covenant, just as all praying is not prayer. Covenant prayers are God and man united in Christ; they are mutually responsible relationships working towards one goal – God's will. Prayer is a relationship of mutual trust in each other's words.

The New Covenant

And what of today? The book of Hebrews tells us that we have a *better* covenant. Hebrews 10:9 says, 'He taketh away the first that he may establish the second'. Under the old covenant, men could walk with God, but under the new covenant, it is 'Christ in you, the hope of glory'. God said to Jeremiah, '. . . I will put my laws in their inward parts, and write it in their hearts . . .' (Jer. 31:33). This is the new birth; now God lives *in* man, not *with* man.

In the old covenant God remembered Abraham, Isaac and Jacob when answering prayer, but in the new He remembers Jesus, the Christ.

In the old covenant God swore to Abraham, but in the new God made an oath to Jesus that He would keep His word. Hebrews 6:17–18 says, 'Wherein God, willing more abundantly to show unto the heirs of promise (that's us) the immutability of his counsel, confirmed it by an oath: That by two immutable things (God the Father and Jesus) in which it was impossible for God to lie, we MIGHT HAVE A STRONG CONSOLATION . . .'. Remember when God the Father turned to Jesus and said, 'Thy throne, O God, is for ever and ever' (Heb. 1:8 KJV) and 'Thou are a priest for ever after the order of Melchizedek' (Heb. 5:6 KJV). Jesus is now the High Priest officiating over the new covenant that God swore He would keep. Jesus is at the right hand of the Father, making intercession for us, and the foundation of His prayers is the new covenant. Jesus is the Will and Testament and Covenant of God. That's what the writer to the Hebrews means when he says that Jesus is the surety or guarantee of the new covenant. He cannot deny Himself.

This unprecedented document of mercy has been drawn up by the Godhead and signed by the divine blood of Jesus, the Lamb. The old covenant is based upon the blood of animals, but the new covenant is based upon the blood of Jesus Christ. Hebrews 13:20–21 in the Living Bible says, '. . . May He who became the great Shepherd of the sheep by our everlasting agreement between God and you, signed with His blood . . .'

What greater assurance can God give to us beyond His oath, His promise and His sacrifice? This everlasting covenant is the 'anchor of the soul' (Heb. 6:19), the end of all uncertainty. No longer do we have to be tossed to and fro with doubts and fear. Now we can, 'come boldly unto the throne of grace, that we may obtain mercy, and find grace to help in time of need' (Heb. 4:16). A revelation of the covenant will thrust your prayers into the realm of 'all things are possible to him that believeth' (Mark 9:23).

Have you joined the family of God? Is Jesus Christ Lord of your life? Then you are a partaker of the covenant just as much as you are a partaker of His divine nature. Galatians 3:29 tells us, 'And if ye be Christ's, then are ye Abraham's seed and heirs according to the promise'. Once you become part of the family of God, you also become a recipient of the covenant because the blessings of the Abrahamic covenant found their fulfilment in Christ, the seed of Abraham, and you have become part of the Seed. You have been joined to Christ. You have put on Christ. All that remains is for you to accept it, believe it, live it and pray it. The blessings of Abraham and the blesings of Jesus are one and they are yours. Isaiah says, 'Everyone that thirsteth, come ye, buy, and eat; yea, come, buy wine and milk, without money and without price . . . and I *will* make an everlasting covenant with you, even the sure mercies of David' (Is. 55:1,3).

The oath, the promise and the sacrifice have been proven to you and all mankind. 'For God so loved the world that he gave his only begotten Son . . .' (John 3:16). God has now provided Himself a Lamb. He has given ALL. He has proved Himself and His word that He will fulfil His covenant. Romans 8:32 says, 'He that spared not his only Son, but gave him up for us all, how shall he not with him also freely give us *all* things'. Since God has given His Son as proof of His love and word, why would He not answer your prayers! As God gave Abraham His word, He gave us His Son. They are the same. And herein lies the mystery of our union. When we stand on our covenant prayers we are standing in Christ. This is why we like Abraham are drawn into union with Christ through covenant praying. When Ezekiel spoke to the dry bones and they came to life, he became the mouthpiece for God's creative power. When Joshua commanded the sun and moon to stand still he was sharing in God's majestic sovereignty. When Mary prayed, 'Be it unto me according to thy word', she became a partner to God's divine wisdom. When Jesus was born in Bethlehem, God shared in man's humanity. Let there be no mistake. Man can never become God, though God became man. Yet as Paul Billheimer writes, 'God has exalted redeemed humanity to such a sublime height that it is impossible for Him to elevate them further without breaching the Godhead.'

'Now to Abraham and his SEED were the promises made . . . And if YE be Christ's, then are YE Abraham's SEED . . .' (Gal. 3:16, 29). Covenant prayers will make real your union with Christ Jesus, and your union with Christ will make real your covenant prayers.

The B.I.B.L.E.
Yes, that's the book for me, I
stand alone on the word of God
the B.I.B.L.E.

Chapter 5

Prayer and Faith
The Dynamic Duo

Faith – The Master Key

Faith is the master key to prayer; it unlocks the door to all of God's marvellous grace. Are we not staggered by the carte blanche God sets before us through prayer and faith? 'If ye have faith as a grain of mustard seed, ye shall say unto this mountain, Remove hence to yonder place: and it shall remove, and *nothing* shall be impossible unto you' (Mt. 17:20 KJV). 'Therefore I say unto you, *What things soever* ye desire, when ye pray, believe that ye receive them and ye shall have them' (Mark 11:24 KJV). 'And this is the confidence that we have in him, that, if we ask *any thing*, according to his will, he heareth us: And if we know that he hear us, whatsoever we ask, we know that we have the petitions that we desire of him' (1 John 5:14–15 KJV).

The scope of our asking in faith is only limited by His word, and has He not said unto us, 'According as his divine power hath given unto us ALL things that pertain unto life and godliness . . .' (1 Pet. 1:3 KJV). Whatever the need is regarding our spiritual development and natural life on earth, He has said, 'only believe!'

Faith cannot operate outside the word of God, for faith 'cometh by hearing and hearing by the word' (Rom. 10:17). The word of God is the soil for faith. Like a seed, unless it is in the right soil it cannot grow.

Continually throughout His word, the Lord focuses a single truth upon our hearts: faith always produces results. Never once do we see faith fail to receive its heart's desire. In every case Jesus would answer, '. . . as thou hast

42

believed, so be it done unto thee . . .' (Mt. 8:13 KJV). 'And Jesus, seeing their faith . . . said . . . Arise and walk' (Mt. 9:2, 5 KJV). 'Daughter, be of good comfort, thy faith hath made thee whole' (Mt. 9:22). 'According to your faith, be it unto you' (Mt. 9:29 KJV).

Jesus moved in response to the cry of faith and answered their prayer. It mattered not whether it was a housewife, a soldier, a beggar or a king, faith resulted in the same end, the answer!

The God-Kind of Faith

This is heart-faith, the God-kind of faith that Jesus told His disciples to have in Mark 11:22. This is not simply an intellectual acceptance of a set of principles or a psychological understanding of certain concepts, but rather this kind of faith is a divinely inspired attribute of God birthed into the human spirit by the Holy Spirit and God's infallible word.

When this kind of faith, God's faith, is actively alive in your heart, you will no longer stagger, even as Abraham didn't, at the promises of God. There is no enemy that can stand before this faith. It has 'subdued kingdoms, worked righteousness, obtained promises, stopped the mouths of lions, quenched the violence of fire, escaped the edge of the sword. Individuals were made strong, people became valiant in battle, turning to flight the armies of the aliens, and women received their dead raised to life again . . .' (Heb. 11:33–35 TLB).

The Bible is one continuous flowing river of God's faith, springing from the hearts of people birthing miracles and wonders. David, a man full of faith asks nature a question, 'What ails you, O sea, that you fled? O Jordan that you hurried back? O mountains, that you skipped like rams? O little hills like lambs? Who turned the rock into a pool of water, the flint into a fountain of waters' (Ps. 114:5–6, 8 KJV). What ails nature? *Faith*! Not the Red Sea nor the Jordan, not the barren desert nor the mountains could resist the power of faith. It will separate you from all others. The Israelites crossed the Red Sea by faith, but the Egyptians drowned. The three Hebrew children walked in the fiery furnace, but the soldiers were consumed. Daniel spent many hours in the lion's den, but the wicked administrators only fifteen seconds. Faith ushers you from the natural into the supernatural, from man's finite into God's infinite, from religion into vital union with Christ. Faith makes Jesus the 'I AM' to you. Faith is the answer to your prayers.

Prayer without faith is like a marriage without love. It's the hidden spark of a living relationship with God. It is the fountain of confidence, the springboard of praise, the shout of triumph! Faith is as much a part of prayer as the echo is to the original sound.

As a heart pours its prayer *out* to God, God will pour His faith back *into* it. It's a complete cycle, just as the rain falls to earth and is evaporated back up, so only as God's faith is recived into our spirits, can we then, 'come boldly before the throne of grace, that we may obtain mercy and find grace to help in time of need' (Heb. 4:16 KJV).

Our whole relationship with God, our union with Christ, our entire prayer life is dependent upon faith, 'for without faith it is impossible to please God' (Heb. 11:6 KJV). And so the question arises, do I have this God-kind faith? The answer is YES! At some point in your life you chose to receive Jesus Christ as your Saviour, and it was then that God gave you a measure of faith to be born again. 'For by grace are ye saved through faith and not of yourselves, it is a gift of God' (Eph. 2:9 KJV). It took God's kind of faith for you to be born again, and that is the wondrous grace of it all. He gave you this faith because of His grace, so you could receive Him, Paul says in Gal. 2:20, '. . . and the life that I now live, I live by the faith *of the Son of God*.'

And just as this faith originated from Him, so must it live by Him. Jesus said, 'If ye *abide* in me and my words abide in you, ye shall ask what you will and it shall be done' (John 15:7 KJV). It is only as we abide in Him, 'the author and finisher of our faith', that this measure of faith will continually produce fruit. He is the 'Life-Giving Spirit, the 'Prince of Life', the 'River of Life'. He is El-Shaddai and, therefore, whatever he gives He sustains. Our faith cannot survive any more than a seed can grow and develop into a plant without the germ of life in it.

Listen to the confession of the lady with the issue of blood, as she said, 'If I may but touch his clothes, I shall be whole' (Mark 5:28 KJV). Her attention was on Jesus, the focus of her faith was on Jesus. The moment of healing came when she was able to touch Jesus.

When your faith is alive, you know that you know that you know the answer is yours. There are no questions for faith has seen the answer. So real and concrete is faith that the writer to the Hebrews says, 'it is the *substance* of things hoped for, the *evidence* of things not seen' (Heb. 11:1 KJV). The Amplified Bible further elaborates on this verse, stating, 'Now faith is the assurance (the confirmation, the title deed) of the things (we) hope for, being the *proof* of things (we) do not see and the *conviction* of their reality – Faith perceiving as *real fact* what is *not revealed to the* senses'.

When faith has risen in your heart, you can rise up from your knees for the battle is over, the answer is yours. Like the nobleman in the fourth chapter of John, you can, 'go thy way, thy son liveth' (John 4:50 KJV). You can descend into the valley and face Goliath because, like David, you know, 'He will give you into our hands' (1 Sam. 17:47 KJV).

When my wife and I first started stepping out on the waters of faith, we encountered a financial crisis. My wife was pregnant with our second child, and the bill of $1,000 was due for the obstetrician that day. We had no money, and we had already decided to trust in God alone and not make our needs known. There was no recourse, we had set our hand to the plough and were not going back. I remember that day clearly, for after two hours of prayer, faith sprang up in my heart, and I knew we had the money. I was still in my prayer closet and could not see the money, but I knew by faith that we had it.

I asked the Lord what had happened, being young in faith, and He quickened Mark 4:28, 'For the earth bringeth forth fruit of herself; first the blade, then the ear, after that the full corn in the ear'. The God-kind of faith that He had planted in my heart at salvation was growing until now it had spring up as a *blade*. Faith was finally discernible to my spirit man. I could see it, feel it and know it. It was more real, more believable, more convincing than the crisis was. I left the office full of joy, and, as I walked through the front door of our house, I was about to give a shout of victory when my wife turned to me with a cheque for $1,085.00. Somebody had stopped by the house and given it to my wife while I was in prayer. Faith cries, 'God answers prayer!'

Jesus constantly intertwined faith with prayer. When the man with the demon-possessed son came to the Lord, his prayers were acceptable; it was his faith that needed to be exercised. Jesus said, 'If thou canst *believe*, all things are possible to him that believeth'. (Mark 9:23 KJV). With the word spoken to him, his faith now reaches through his unbelief, and his son is delivered. How many prayers had he prayed before, how many times had he cried out in desperation, but now, like rain to a barren land, his faith *broke through* the once hardened soil and blossomed. His son had been healed. Faith brought substance to his prayers.

When the disciples marveled at how Jesus caused the fig tree to wither, He answered them, 'therefore I say unto you, what things soever ye desire *when ye pray*, *believe* that ye receive them, and ye shall *have them*' (Mk. 11:24). He was saying that the salient ingredient of prayer is believing.

Faith – Energized Prayer

In Luke 11, Jesus is teaching His disciples on prayer by giving them the example of a person who goes to his friend's house at midnight and knocks on the door, asking for some bread. The friend is not inclined to get up at midnight, rummage through the kitchen for the loaves, unlock the door and give them to him. But, because of this person's importunity, or relentless persistence, the friend knows he will not go away until he gets the bread. This is the power of faith in prayer; it will enable you to persist with relentless energy until the answer comes. This is why Jesus says, 'Ask and it *shall* be given you, seek and ye *shall* find, knock and it *shall* be opened unto you (Luke 11:9 KJV).

Faith not only brings the answer, but enables us to continue in prayer.

How many battles have been lost because prayer was offered up with no faith. The only difference in the acceptability of the sacrifices (which represent our prayers) of Cain and Abel was faith. When Lazarus was sick, Mary and Martha called upon the Lord in prayer, but Lazarus died and their prayers were muffled in a sea of heartbreak. It was then that the Lord walked in on the scene. Yet for Mary and Martha all hope was gone, all possibilities were vanquished, all prayers were futile. At seeing Jesus, they both said, 'Lord, if thou hadst been here, my brother had not died' (John 11:21 KJV). In their minds, Jesus had not answered prayer and they stopped believing, yet to this Jesus says to Martha, '. . .if thou wouldest *believe*, thou shouldest see the glory of God' (John 11:40 KJV). Yes, believe, for even now it was not too late. Over and over Jesus would say to man's unbelief, '. . . wherefore didst thou doubt, O ye of little faith'.

Have you given up in prayer? Has your faith been crushed by time and circumstance? Then look afresh at the King of Glory and know that He is the author and finisher of your faith. It is only in seeing Him that faith lives, for He is the fountainhead of our believing.

For Peter and Jairus this proved to be true.

Peter found himself being overcome by the storm and the frightful prospect of dying at sea. The winds were howling, the waves rising, the lightning crackling. Peter was sinking into the sea and his world had become a coffin lid about to be shut. Fear and desperation had gripped his soul. In his great distress, Peter called out in prayer, 'Lord, save me!'

At another time, Jairus was standing near Jesus. Hope draining from his soul, bleeding as only a father's heart could, he looked at Jesus. Gloom swirled around his spirit, his mind frozen as the words, 'Your daughter is dead' echoed down every corridor of his consciousness.

Surely these two men had reason to fear, and would not doubt and depression be normal in situations such as these? Yet Jesus interrupts the natural and *breaks through* into their world of darkness as the resurrection and the life by saying to Peter, 'Why are ye fearful, O ye of little faith?' (Mt. 8:26 KJV). And to Jairus, 'Fear not, believe only, and she shall be made whole' (Luke 8:50 KJV).

Clearly Jesus was calling them out of the natural, out of the normal, out of the human shroud and into the heights of faith where the miraculous is experienced. It was faith, ever-living faith, ever-abundant faith that Jesus was telling them to add to their prayers, and it is the same for today's prayer warriors. Listen to Him whisper to you, child of prayer, 'Fear not little flock, for it is your Father's good pleasure to give you the Kingdom' (Lk. 12:32).

Faith seizes His Kingdom, whereas our nature cannot inherit it. And prayer (as sacred an exercise as it is) is only human unless touched by the Master's gift of faith, which dwells in the heart of every believer. Remember, faith and prayer are God and man in union in Christ, establishing His Kingdom on earth.

The person who has learned to pray the prayer of faith stands unshakeable, undisturbed and unapologetic. He is rooted and grounded in Christ, and though the world may be chaotic, his inner faith serves as an internal, divine bulwark against all external maladies. As Jesus stood untouched in the midst of the raging Sea of Galilee, so can you, 'be still, and know that he is God' (Ps. 46:10 KJV), in the centre of a hostile world. The Psalmist writes in Psalm 46:1–3:

God is our refuge and strength
A very present help in trouble.
Therefore we will not fear,
Though the earth be removed,
And though the mountains be carried
into the midst of the sea;
Though the waters thereof roar and be troubled,
Though the mountains shake with the swelling thereof.

The man of faith says, 'He will not be afraid of evil tidings; his heart is steadfast, trusting in the Lord' (Ps. 112:7 NKJV).

Faith is the divine witness that propels you from a life of religious theology into the Who's Who of the eleventh chapter of Hebrews. Like them, you can endure because you

48

are, 'seeing him who is invisible' (Heb. 11:27 KJV). It was faith that inspired Abraham to pray for 25 years, and it is faith that will be the ballast for your prayer life. It was faith that allowed Jesus to see on the otherside of the grave the countless multitudes who would accept Him as their Saviour, and faith will allow you to do the same, to *see*, to *know*, to *receive*. In God's realm, believing comes first, then the receiving.

Prayer says, 'show me thy path'

Faith says, 'You *are* my path.'

Can you not hear the Spirit of the Lord say, 'Come up hither'? Like Moses, let us climb up Mount Zion, leaving the multitude of doubters behind us until we reach the cleft of the rock and safely abide in the God of 'all things are possible!'

Chapter 6

Prayer and the Holy Spirit

Identification With Christ

As I was driving to work one morning through the beautiful Malibu mountains in California, enjoying a time of praise with the Lord, a song rose up out of my spirit, and I started to sing:

I want to know You in the trueness of Your Spirit,
To touch You, to see You, to hear You.
That I may live within Your life,
That I'll abide within Your presence.
I want to know You in the trueness of Your Spirit.

It was a prophetic song, for it was not until some years later that I realized the only true way to know Jesus is by the Spirit. Paul said in 2 Corinthians 5:16, 'Wherefore henceforth know we no man after the flesh: yea, though we have known Christ after the flesh, yet now henceforth know we Him no more'.

The disciples, like Paul, had seen, heard and even touched Jesus when He walked in the flesh. But their true understanding of who He was became clear following Pentecost. This is why Jesus said to His disciples, 'Nevertheless I tell you the truth. It is to your ADVANTAGE that I go away, for if I do not go away, the Helper will not come to you: but if I depart, I will send Him to you' (John 16:7 NKJV).

The advantage is that now we can be united to Christ, spirit to Spirit by the Holy Spirit, allowing Christ's life to become our life. When Jesus was in the flesh, His disciples could only see Jesus hanging on the cross, being crucified and dying. They could only witness the fact that Jesus rose from the dead and ascended to heaven. But once the Holy Spirit came, He took this historic, redemptive event called Calvary and made it a present-day, first person reality to the disciples.

For ten days the disciples prepared themselves through prayer to receive the promised gift from Jesus. And when the Holy Spirit came, He joined them to Christ. Now they saw THEMSELVES going to Calvary with Christ, being placed upon the cross and crucified with Christ to the world, the flesh and temptation. Then they saw themselves die together with Christ to sin.

But wonder of wonders, the journey did not end there. They were then raised with Christ from the dead to 'newness of life' as victors, conquerors and overcomers, even as Christ is over all the enemies of God. In a final chain of divine splendour, the Holy Spirit seated them with Christ at the right hand of the Father in power and authority, where they reign with Christ. Is it any mystery then that they did the same works as Jesus? And the Holy Spirit will do the same with us as we spend time in prayer.

The Word and the Holy Spirit eternally work as one, which is why we need to know Christ, 'in the trueness of the Spirit, to touch Him, to see Him, and hear Him, that we may live within His life and abide within His presence'. As John writes, 'And hereby we know that he abideth in us, by the Spirit which he hath given us' (John 3:24 KJV).

Prayer is the mother's womb in which the Holy Spirit births our *identification* with Christ. As the Spirit moves within this prayer womb, we become familiar with His voice and His touch, His ways and leadings. He inspires trust and obedience. He instructs, corrects, and reveals until we awake with the likeness of Christ. 'We are fearfully and wonderfully made' (Ps. 139:14) in this prayer womb.

Listening to the Holy Spirit

Jesus said, 'My sheep hear my voice . . . and they follow

me': That is the voice of the Spirit speaking the word. Therefore, walking in the Spirit is following Jesus and keeping His word. This is how our walk with Christ becomes more intimate and accurate.

The Holy Spirit takes the things of Christ and shows them unto us (John 16:15). Paul understood this when he wrote, 'For as many as are led by the Spirit of God, they are the sons of God' (Rom. 8:14). Through this process, we become doers of the word because we know by the Spirit what to do.

The Apostles' success came because through prayer they learned to have a relationship with the Holy Spirit even as Jesus did. And this is where our success comes also, walking in the Spirit (which is communion with the Holy Spirit) even as Jesus walked in the Spirit. Paul writes, 'But I say, walk and live habitually in the (Holy) Spirit, responsive to and controlled and guided by the Spirit. Then you will certainly not gratify the cravings and desires of the flesh, of human nature without God' (Gal. 5:16 AMP).

Jesus, The Son of God, as The Son of Man was completely yielded to the Holy Spirit. It was the Holy Spirit who drove Jesus into the wilderness, who instructed Him to fast for 40 days, to walk on the water, to pray through the night, to meet the woman of Samaria by the well at a certain time. It was the Holy Spirit who led Jesus to the upper room, who placed Him upon the cross (Heb. 9:14), and who raised Him from the dead, seating Him at the Father's right hand.

The whole life and ministry of Jesus was Spirit led. He said, 'The words that I speak they are Spirit and they are life' (John 6:63). Concerning His emotions, He was 'moved with compassion' (Mt. 9:36), and His works, He did what He did because He said, 'The Spirit of the Lord is upon me' (Luke 4:18). From being formed in the womb of Mary to His glorification, Jesus was Spirit led.

Jesus walked in perfect harmony with the Father because he walked in perfect harmony with the Holy Spirit. This is what He taught His disciples to do. 'But the Helper, the Holy Spirit, whom the Father will send in My name, He will teach you ALL THINGS and bring to your remembrance all things that I said to you' (John 14:26 NKJV).

Praying in and with the Holy Spirit

The Apostles discovered the link between praying IN the Holy Spirit and COMMUNING (which is praying) WITH the Holy Spirit. Paul said, 'I thank my God I speak with tongues more than you all' (1 Cor. 14:18 NKJV). Paul was 'praying always with all prayer and supplication in the Spirit . . .' (Eph. 6:18). Whatever kind of prayer Paul prayed, whether in tongues or in his native language, he endeavoured to pray *in* the Spirit. Even when all languages of angels or of men (1 Cor. 13:1) failed in communicating his heart, he found that, 'The Spirit also helpeth our infirmities (natural limitations) for we know not what we should pray for as we ought: but the Spirit itself maketh intercession for us with groanings which cannot be uttered' (Rom. 8:33).

Without the Holy Spirit we could not pray aright. I can remember a time when there was a quiet pricking of my conscience warning me that I may be diverting from God's perfect will. Since it came and went with no real discomfort I did not make it a matter of prayer. Then one day as I was praying in the Spirit I felt compelled to ask the Lord for the interpretation. The answer was a surprising revelation.

I was praying in other tongues for what I would not pray for in English, which was to 'cleanse my heart from doing things my way!' By praying in tongues God was able to answer the intercession of the Holy Spirit in me and a work of grace was done. It made a marked difference in my ministry from that day forward and gave me cause for great joy because of the purifying of my heart.

When we pray in the Spirit we are speaking mysteries. In those moments we can be praying in agreement with many we may not agree with in the natural. Disagreement over certain doctrines is one of the greatest causes of disunity in prayer throughout the body of Christ. Praying in the Spirit, however, enables us to join our faith with people we may not otherwise pray with.

The Lord has spoken to my wife and I to hold a crusade in Birmingham, England, in the Winter of 1985. Three days following the Lord's words to us I awoke with a debilitating sickness so severe I could not get out of bed. I had only three weeks to put together an entire crusade and sickness was not on the agenda. It was clearly an attack from the devil because the name of the place where we were to hold the crusade was Druid's Heath. However, 9,000 miles away intercession was going up by my sister-in-law, who by the Spirit knew we were experiencing demonic oppression. Her letter arrived two weeks later explaining why she had prayed for us. It was 'spot on' as they say in England. Because of her intercession the sickness was broken, the crusade was a success and Druid's Heath was turned into Gloryland for three unforgettable days as many lives were changed by the power of God.

Oh that the Church would see that praying in the Holy Spirit is not some antiquated ecclesiastic exercise but rather a divinely appointed weapon to be held in the hands of Kingdom heroes!

When Jesus stood before Lazarus' tomb, He 'groaned in the Spirit' (John 11:33). Paul was in 'travail' over the Galatian and Thessalonian Christians until Christ was formed in them (Gal 4:19, 1 Thess. 2:9).

Praying in the Spirit will keep you sensitive to His voice.

It will build your faith. Jude said, 'But ye, beloved, building up yourselves on your most holy faith, praying in the Holy Ghost' (Jude 14).

It is one of God's ways of making His will known. As Paul prayed in the Spirit, the will of the Holy Spirit was revealed and soon churches were birthed in other lands, even while Paul was in prison.

It releases us to minister. The Apostle John was able to minister to seven churches in Asia while a prisoner on the Isle of Patmos. Praying in the Spirit accomplishes the task in the spirit realm which then makes it possible for us to carry it out in the natural realm. We must ever be mindful that God came before man, that spirit comes before flesh, and so prayer comes before action.

Fellowship-ing or praying with the Holy Spirit will bring life to your prayer words even as the words of Jesus were Spirit and life. There are many prayer failures because the words are not anointed. They are lifeless and dead. We must let the Holy Spirit catch away our words even as He caught Philip away and placed him where he wanted him to be. 'So shall My word be that goeth forth out of my mouth; it shall not return unto me void, but it shall accomplish that which I please, and it shall prosper in the things whereto I SEND it' (Is. 55:11). Christ's mouth and words become our mouth and words when we pray, 'not by might nor by power, but by my Spirit' (Zec. 4:6).

When we pray in the Spirit, there are no prayer failures, for the Holy Spirit becomes the Prayer Warrior in us. As He anointed Samson to slay a thousand Philistines with the jaw bone of a donkey, so will He empower us to slay a host of demons with the word of God. Like David, He will gird you up with strength to run through a troop of principalities and rulers of darkness as well, or to leap over any wall of spiritual wickedness in high places. You will cut down Goliath and be counted as one of the mighty men of David!

The Holy Spirit is the Greater One within you. He is the might and power of the Lord, the exceeding greatness of His power that raised Christ from the dead. He *is* Pentecost, He *is* God! When you work with Him in prayer like Jesus, you will walk into the synagogue of life and drive out the money changers. He is boldness!

The Holy Spirit desires the same relationship with us, even as He had with Jesus, The Son of Man. He wants to work through us even as He did through Jesus. But this can only be developed through prayer, that essential key to communion.

He is God and has a will. He has desires as well as certain ways of accomplishing the building of Christ's Kingdom. The disciples knew the difference between the voice of the Father (Mt. 3:17), the Son (Acts 10: 13,15) and the Holy Spirit (Acts 10:19). Philip the Evangelist also knew the voice of the Holy Spirit. Acts 8:29 says,'Then the Spirit said to Philip, "Go near and overtake this chariot"'. The Apostle Paul also knew the difference, for Jesus spoke to him at his conversion, and the Holy Spirit spoke to him forbidding him to preach in Asia.

Since the Holy Spirit is God and a Person, we need to

commune with Him. Paul writes, 'The grace of the Lord Jesus Christ and the love of God and the *communion* of the Holy Spirit be with you all. Amen' (2 Cor. 13:14 NKJ). Prayer is communing, sharing, discussing, listening, and this is the fellowship the Holy Spirit desires with us. John tells us in 1 John 2:27 that the Holy Spirit abides in us and we in Him. The abiding is mutual. Man and the Holy Spirit are communicating to maintain the relationship. We can call this friendship.

The Divine Link

Through prayer and the Holy Spirit, we go from the theological fact of being 'in Christ' to living and *experiencing* our 'union with Christ'. His nature, mind and character are revealed in and through us by the Spirit. The head is what gives direction, organization and information to the body, but there must be a nervous system by which these messages are carried. This is one of the functions of the Holy Spirit. In turn, the body needs to send stimuli to the head, informing it of its needs. This is prayer. These three work together, creating a union.

I minister because the Holy Spirit anoints me; I pray because He motivates me. I exercise by running because I 'feel His pleasure'. I have learned to follow the Head, the Word, by the Spirit. The nervous system has linked the head and the body so that a union can be formed. Now we can walk in harmony with Christ, the head, as we walk in harmony with the Spirit . . . and the miraculous mechanism that makes it possible is prayer.

Many reject and quench the Holy Spirit because they want to do what they desire to do, rather than what Jesus wants. Hence, they avoid prayer. Yet Paul writes to us about this by saying, 'What? know ye not that your body is the temple of the Holy Spirit which is in you, which ye have of God, and ye are not your own? For ye are bought with a price: therefore glorify God in your body, and in your spirit, which are God's' (1 Cor. 6:19–20). Like Jesus, we now surrender to the leading of the Spirit and allow Him to take us where He desires, even to the cross.

I will never forget the day the Holy Spirit spoke to me, saying, 'Your body belongs to me'. How wonderfully true this has become over the years. My feet now go where He leads me. My mouth now speaks His words. My eyes and ears see and hear what He wants me to see and hear. My heart is filled with His love, my mind with His peace. He has filled me with Himself. My members are now instruments of righteousness, as I yield to Him.

He will shed abroad the love of God in your heart, even as he moved Jesus with compassion. He will form Christ in you even as He formed Christ in Mary's womb. He will reveal the mind of Christ even as He revealed the Father's mind to Jesus. This is relationship. This is prayer.

So many churches and individuals are afraid of the Holy Spirit because they do not understand Him, even though He has been here almost 2,000 years, while Jesus was on earth only 33½ years. Yet, knowing the Holy Spirit was the secret of Christ's walk with His Father, the success of the early church, and the only way we can truly know Jesus Christ and worship the Father (John 4:24).

Deep is calling unto deep, Spirit is calling unto spirit. Can you not hear Him calling you . . .

Therefore, if there is any consolation in Christ, if any comfort of love, if any FELLOWSHIP *of the Spirit* . . . fulfil my joy being like-minded, having the same mind, being of one accord, of one mind.

(Phil. 2:1–2)

Chapter 7

Prayer
A Loving Interlude

What Doth Hinder You?

The Father has torn away the veil to His throne-room by the atoning work of His Son. Our hearts have been cleansed, we are now clothed with white robes of righteousness, we have been 'accepted into the beloved' and have been brought into union with Christ. The work is complete.

The question now comes, 'what doth hinder you?' In God's eyes there is nothing; His love casts out all fear, His mercy remembers your sins no more, His Son has removed God's wrath, and His Word declares, 'Yet the proof of God's amazing love is this: that it was while we were sinners that Christ died for us. Moreover, if He did that for us while we were sinners, now that we are men justified by the shedding of His blood, what reason have we to fear the wrath of God? If, while we were His enemies, Christ reconciled us to God by dying for us, surely now that we are reconciled, we may be *perfectly certain* of our salvation through His *living in us*' (Rom. 5:8–11 JBP).

Surely, if Jesus Christ is able to live in us or be in our presence because of God's reconciliation to us, then we are able to live in His presence. That is our door to prayer – actually abiding within one another – union.

When one experiences this union with Christ, then one also experiences forgiveness in Christ, and together they form a time of prayer when God and man can come together for a loving interlude.

This is a time when love is the fragrance of your

communion with the Father. Your sins, fears and insecurities have been put aside, and you can enjoy God. He is your Father and you are His son or daughter. Your time with Him fills you with peace and joy. You feel welcome and at ease.

How David understood this kind of loving prayerful relationship with the Father! Listen to his abundant joy as he enters into his prayer closet and writes, 'Make a joyful noise unto the Lord . . ., serve the Lord with gladness, come before His presence with singing, enter into His gates with thanksgiving, and into His courts with praise' (Ps. 100:1,2,4 KJV). David was completely honest and open as he drew away from his work and entered into his time with God. It was a loving interlude, not a time of formal rituals or memorized confessions void of life, but rather a sharing of hearts. David understood, 'in Thy presence is the fullness of joy, and at Thy right hand are pleasures evermore' (Ps. 16:11 KJV). David was of a different breed, for he loved God with all of his heart and felt comfortable with Him.

David shouted, 'He forgiveth ALL thine iniquities and healeth all thy diseases' (Ps. 103:3 NKJV). With all his sins 'cast into the sea of forgetfulness', David comes to only one conclusion about our heavenly Father, 'How precious also are Thy thoughts unto me' (Ps. 139:17). David knew the Father thought loving thoughts about Him and all mankind, and, because of this, he trusted God completely. No wonder he was a man of faith and praise. He trusted his Father to protect, save and lead him. In turn, David deeply respected, loved and served God.

The Flame of Love

What a privilege it was for Solomon to be nurtured in such an environment of prayer. Solomon saw the love between David and Jehovah, and in time Solomon's prayer life is witnessed in the Song of Solomon. It is a love song birthed out of intimacy with God.

It is sad, however, that Solomon lost his first love with our heavenly Father, which resulted in excesses. But what of the Church today? How many have grown cold? How many cry, 'prayer is a vain thing'? I believe the relationships of David and Solomon are prophetic of Church history. Like David, when the Church was first birthed in the Book of Acts, devotion to Jesus Christ knew no bounds, 'not death nor life, nor angels, nor principalities, nor powers, nor things present, nor things to come, nor height, nor depth, nor any other creature could separate (them) from the *love* of God, which is Christ Jesus (the) Lord' (Rom. 8:38-39). A romance of unquenchable fire was aflame in the hearts of early Christians, and, like David, their love for God made them valiant and daring. Their war cry against evil was sparked in their love for Christ.

But time introduced new generations, and, like Solomon, their hearts grew cold. Life and religion became a vain thing. However, the eternal flame of God's love is never daunted, and He has promised through His prophets that He will restore the house of David to twice as much glory. It is time for the restoration of David's house! It is time for the Church to enter into its prayer closet and experience the love of God.

The enemy of our soul has declared war on the saints, and the forces of darkness are being unleashed in an unprecedented way. How can we go to battle without love, without knowing He will never leave us nor forsake us, that love never fails, that His banner over us is love! Where there is no love, there is no cause. Where there is no cause, there is no battle. Where there is no battle, the enemy has won. What did Jesus tell His disciples before he went to Calvary? 'Greater *love* hath no man than this, that a man lay down his life for his friends' (John 15:3 KJV). It was because of love that Jesus entered and won the battle for your soul. Dear Reader, the Father is calling you back to this prayer relationship of love. Oh, now he desires amid the chaotic upheavals of life to have a loving interlude with you!

God is not all work and no play; God is not a driving taskmaster, forcing His people on to perfection. Rather, He wants us to draw aside and enjoy our fellowship with Him, to bask in His companionship.

Drawing Aside

How often we read of Jesus drawing aside for prayer. I do not believe He prayed only about ministry, but there were times when the Father and Son expressed their divine love for each other. Hear the Father say, 'This is my *beloved* Son, in whom I am well pleased' (Mt. 3:17 KJV). Jesus, when answering the Jews said, 'I and my Father are one' (John 10:30 KJV), and again He says, 'the Father is *in* me, and I in Him' (John 10:38 KJV). Jesus and the Father were abiding in a loving interlude, which is what He is calling us to do. Does not Paul declare, 'but ye have received the Spirit of adoption, whereby we cry, 'Abba, Father' (Rom. 8:15 KJV). God has now become *our* Father through our union with Christ. Imagine, you and Jesus have the same Father. This is grace, this is mercy, this is the depth of the love of Christ.

When the disciples asked Jesus to teach them how to pray, the Lord first taught them to say, 'Our Father . . . (Mt. 6:9 KJV). Even here Jesus was revealing that prayer is not an empty ritual but a relationship of intimate love. Continually Jesus was communicating to them that union with Christ brings fellowship with the Father.

In this relationship of prayer, we can share not only our love, joys and victories, but our sorrows, hurts, disappointments and failures. Within this loving relationship, we can share out of trust, knowing He will turn our sorrows into joy, our mourning into dancing and our ashes into beauty.

Beloved Church, we are the bride of Christ, adorned with His righteousness, glory and honor, and being a bride is the height of the romance, the culmination of the courtship. It is when your love has brought you to the place where the two become one. As the two of you stand before each other, you will exchange vows of love, forever pledging yourself to a life of intimacy, to a life of prayer.

Once you have fallen in love and experienced this union with Christ, there is no turning back. You have stepped out on the water and there is only Jesus and yourself. As Peter walked towards Jesus, he failed. The storm moved him from faith to fear and so he sank in the waters of doubt. But when Jesus picked him up and they walked arm and arm back together, Peter did not fail. He was walking WITH CHRIST. They were in union; now Peter could not fail as long as he walked with Christ. The storm was still raging, the wind still blowing, the waves still swelling, but none of it mattered for Jesus and Peter walked as one back to the boat. Would Peter ever let go of Christ walking back? No! Christ had become his life, his Saviour, his peace, his confidence, his all in all, as they walked over the turbulent sea. Peter's heart as they walked back together is aptly described by Solomon, '. . . I found Him whom my soul loveth: I held Him, and would not let Him go . . .' (S. of S. 3:4 KJV).

Dear reader, will you not step out on the water? Will you not walk out in faith as you hear the Master calling? Look not at the storm. Listen not to the winds nor be moved by the waves, but look only to Jesus. '. . . the author and finisher of our faith . . .' and walk! (Heb. 12;12 KJV). Trust Him, for not only can He bring us to Himself, but He can keep us also.

Are you afraid that you will fall in the waters? Many have, but Jesus is standing there to pull you out. Solomon wrote, 'By night on my bed I sought him whom my soul loveth: I sought him, but I found him not. I will rise now, and go about the city in the streets, and in the broad ways I will seek him whom my soul loveth: I sought him, but I found him not. The watchmen that go about the city found me: to whom I said, Saw ye him whom my soul loveth? It was a little that I passed from them, *but I found Him whom my soul loveth*: I held him, and would not let him go, until I had brought him into my mother's house, and into the chamber of her that conceived me' (S. of S. 3:1–4 KJV).

We cannot rest until we enter back into that sweet place of fellowship, even as Peter could not rest until the Lord lifted him out of the water. Love is like nectar to the bee. It draws you. It is essential to life. You are as dependent as the branch is to the vine. 'Abide in me, and I in you. As the branch cannot bear fruit itself, except it abide in the vine: no more can ye, except ye abide in me' (John 15:4 KJV).

So precious is this fellowship and union that it must be carefully preserved through our prayer life. One's spirit becomes sensitive to any changes that may occur in the relationship. Immediately the Spirit longs and calls us to our knees again, even as Peter cried out in the water. Solomon again so aptly describes the heart in this condition, 'I opened to my beloved; but my beloved had withdrawn himself, and was gone: my soul failed when he spake: I sought him, but I could not find him; I called him, but he gave me no answer. The watchmen that went about the city found me, they smote me, they wounded me; the keepers of the walls took away my veil from me. I charge you, O daughters of Jerusalem, if ye find my beloved, that ye tell him, that I am sick of love' (S. of S. 5:6–8 KJV).

Yes, you become sick with love; if somehow you have moved off of faith, and the intimacy of your union with Christ has been clouded. You must find Him again.

It is not a question of losing one's salvation or of Christ leaving you, or even the Father locking the doors to the throne-room, but rather the question of abiding. For it is in abiding in this loving interlude with Christ that we keep our union vital.

Prayer is a bedchamber of quiet listening and joyful expressions of eternal gratitude. Oh, can we not see that when we commit adultery with the world we are inviting another into our bedchamber with our Lord? As a 'house of prayer', we must drive out all invaders from our fellowship with God in Christ. Prayer is sacred. Prayer is holy. Prayer is loving God. The stronger our love grows, the sooner we will shun sin. Solomon said, 'I have taken off my robe; must I put it on again? I have washed my feet; must I soil them again?' (S. of S. 5:3 NIV).

Peter's cry to Jesus was a prayer. Our Saviour's reply was His answer. Have you asked? Then He has answered, 'Come!' Let nothing hinder you for, 'the just shall live by the faith', and 'faith works by love' (Heb. 10:38 KJV), (Gal. 5:6 KJV). Peter found this to be true as he walked toward the Savior in faith; 'Many waters cannot quench love, neither can the floods drown it' (S. of S. 8:7 KJV).

He is calling you into a loving interlude, into union with Christ, and prayer is the incubation chamber that allows the Spirit to make it a reality.

In my heart I heard a voice
calling me away to God's divine choice.
Where love reigns supreme,
and fire, a purifying stream.
Alone with God,
He removed all earthly sod.
Then came heaven's most glorious sight.
The love of Christ – my soul's delight!

D.C.

We have seen how our union with Christ through the new birth, the word, faith, the Holy Spirit, and love becomes and forever remains our basis for answered prayer. Secondly, we have discovered that prayer is the pathway to entering into and living in union with Christ.

From here we can now look at the practical side of prayer, the nitty-gritty of what and how to pray. Be open to discovering hinderances that may be preventing the break through you need in prayer as you read the following chapters.

PART II

The Difference Between Success and Failure in Prayer

Introduction

The compelling question that now arises is, how do I arrive at the place where I desire to pray, pray in harmony with God and pray effectually? The answer is perhaps not what we would like to hear, and yet there is only one way, to pray! The next question, then is, 'What kind of prayer?' Prayer 'without ceasing'!

Enoch was a man who walked with God, and it is of interest to note that his name means 'discipline'. Daily, Enoch would train and discipline himself by the power of the Holy Spirit to pray without ceasing, to walk in continuous fellowship with the Lord, and, as he did, day by day, week by week, year by year, he drew closer and closer until he was in such union with heaven that it was impossible for earth to hold him any longer.

Prayer was the breath of his life as it must be for us. Enoch understood that practice makes perfect. There is no substitute, no short cut, no instant method. Relationships take time.

The following pages were written to enumerate the practical ingredients that form successful prayers. They are life-long building blocks that will enable you to grow in this most vital art of Christian communication, prayer.

Chapter 8

Prayer
A Holy Habit

There is much to be said for the habit of prayer because once the habit is formed it is very difficult to break. The nature of a habit is consistency, faithfulness and the power of determination. This is what will build up your resistance to change, temptation, circumstances, opinions or other forces pressuring you to compromise. The habit of prayer will enable you to stand up under pressure, especially when your habit is sustained and reinforced by the power of the Holy Spirit and the word.

The habit of prayer is like an insurance policy or a security blanket. It is there to carry you through when personal preference or assaults from the enemy attempt to break down your prayer life.

We need, like Enoch, to become so established in our prayer habit that it is harder *not* to pray than it is *to* pray. I can remember when this transition took place in my own life. After I had spent much time in prayer, the Holy Spirit changed my priorities and desires to such a degree that it became contrary to my nature not to pray. Spending time in the presence of the King is so joyfully addictive!

Praying allows God to permeate the very fibre of our spirit, soul and body. Through prayer, our whole being becomes filled with Him, and, therefore, failing to pray has the same consequences as failing to eat. As our bodies become drained of energy, so our spirits will become void of the power of Christ.

A minister who stands before his congregation without having spent those hours in prayer is at best an imitation.

He can only offer the people his words in his own strength. It is like watching a movie – it's real, but it has no life.

Prayerless Christians are not aware of their lethargic spiritual condition, but once you are living in the conscious presence of God, failing to pray is like throwing a car into reverse when moving forward. Prayer has become your nature, your way of life, your secret to walking in union with Christ. To acquiesce with your flesh, the world or the devil would be to send shock waves through your being. Your prayer habit has now become a sensing barometer to the presence of Christ in your life.

When Paul wrote to the Corinthians, he said, 'I beseech you, brethren, (ye know the house of Stephanas, that it is the firstfruits of Achaia, and that they have *addicted* themselves to the ministry of the saints,)' (1 Cor. 16:15 KJV). These believers were so in the habit of giving that they became spiritually addicted to it. We could call this a holy habit.

The same principle applies to prayer. Romans 12:12 (JBP) says, 'When trials come, endure them patiently: *steadfastly maintain the habit of prayer*'. In order for these Roman Christians to maintain the habit of prayer during a crisis, there must have been a habit formed prior to the trial. Many Christians fail in times of testing because they expect a quick fix to their emergency plea for help, but, because there is no habit, no persistence in their prayer life, they soon abandon their pathway to deliverance.

When David was confronted with his adversaries, he said, 'but I give myself unto prayer' (Ps. 109:4 KJV). Paul was reminding the Romans of the same truth. Maintain your prayer life during the trials!

Daniel had developed the habit of praying three times a day. When he was challenged to break that habit he chose prayer over his life. He was determined that nothing would hinder his communion with Almighty God. How precious the prayer habit was to Daniel. How he cherished it, lived for it, devoted himself to it! Prayer was his way of life. It was not a reactionary response to a difficult situation. He was simply praying as he had always prayed.

The early Church was earmarked by the habit of prayer.

Nine o'clock in the morning was commonly referred to as 'the hour of prayer'. Acts 2:42 tells us, 'they continued steadfastly . . . in prayers'. All through the Book of Acts we see prayer at work, a habit that literally served as a foundation for changing the world.

When Paul and Silas were beaten and imprisoned, persecuted and chained for preaching the gospel, the secret of their joy and success is revealed in their response – prayer and praise. How contradictory this is to human nature, but for them, prayer had become their *first nature*.

The prayer habit is not established overnight. It takes time and discipline. The motivation, desire and power will be supplied by the Holy Spirit. But we must turn aside, focus our hearts and minds on the Lord and pray. Prayer produces the fruit of discipline, and discipline helps us to pray.

Before Paul became a Christian, he was already in the habit of prayer. He was, 'zealous towards God' (Acts 27:3). And so, when he was converted, that habit was transferred to his Christian life. A novice could not have fasted and prayed as Paul did at his conversion unless it was his custom already.

The disciples spent ten days in prayer, supplication and praise after Jesus ascended. The reason for this was that for three and a half years the Lord taught them by example and precept in the habit of prayer.

Cornelius, like Paul, was another man who was a 'devout man . . . and prayed to God always' (Acts 10:2 KJV). Once again, God found a man who was prepared to receive because of prayer. Through Cornelius, a man of prayer, came the glorious gospel to the Gentiles.

Developing a Prayer Pattern

Every Christian must establish his own prayer pattern or habit. There is no one formula. God is infinite, flexible and always 'now'. Our prayer life is part of 'working out our salvation . . .' (Phil. 2:12). We are not left to our own, 'for it is God which worketh in you both to *will* and *to do* of His good pleasure' (Phil. 2:13 KJV). With Christ in you, you now have the mind of Christ, and, as you begin to ask God how and when to pray, ideas will come to your mind. This is prayer, and this is God answering.

When I first began to pray, I was in graduate school, working 20 hours a week, and completing my internship, yet I was able to pray three hours a day. After graduation, there was a three month period before starting work as a counsellor, which allowed me to spend six to eight hours a day with the Lord. It was a life-transforming experience. Once working again, I was concerned about my prayer time, but the Lord gave me a promise in Luke 10:42, 'But one things is needful: and Mary hath chosen that good part, which shall not be taken away from her'. Mary had chosen to sit at the feet of Jesus, and, after sitting at the feet of Jesus in prayer, I did not want to leave. His promise to me was, 'it shall not be taken away'.

It was now a question of when to pray. I would arise at 4:30 am and spend two hours with the Lord. While travelling to work, I would pray and praise. Once at work, I would take my breaks and lunch time to meditate and pray. Many times I would forgo fellowship with others and food to spend that time with the Lord. Upon arriving home, I would then spend another two hours with the Lord.

Over the years my schedule has changed, as well as my life's work. Now, a missionary/evangelist, my personal time of prayer has changed. There are many evenings when I am up late, due to ministry, and I may not get to bed before 1:00 or 2:00 am. Arising at 4:30 am is not feasible, nor healthy and wise, but, regardless of when I wake up, I spend the following two to four hours with the Lord. When the afternoon arrives, I can sense the Holy Spirit calling me aside again for an hour or more of prayer.

I have learned that I need a minimum of two hours a day of private prayer to enable me to accomplish God's will and purpose in my own life. Where I am ministering may call for more or less prayer time for effective ministry. As you begin to pray, you will also find your level of need and God's will for your life.

I share this with you not so you will feel obligated to assume this pattern but that you will know that each individual can find time in his schedule to pray. As an evangelist, I have stayed in many homes, some without heat, so getting out of bed in the morning is worthy of the purple heart. Yet I will roll out, bundle myself up and begin to dance before the Lord until I can feel my body. In other places it will be so hot and humid that when you wake up your energy is sapped. This may call for extreme measures, like splashing cold water in your face to wake up!

In various places, there are no vacant rooms to be alone with God; therefore, the outdoors or the car or a closet or a bathroom may have to do. Many times we travel long distances from morning to night to be on time for minstry, which leaves no time for private prayer. I will then have my wife drive so I can concentrate on the Lord for an hour or more. The key is to maintain the habit of prayer, yet be flexible in your given environment.

A Chinese pastor was imprisoned in a concentration camp when the Communists took over the country. He was watched from morning till night, which never allowed him any private time for prayer. He was then assigned to the daily task of cleaning out the camp's cesspool. When he would lift the cover off of the cesspool, the stench was so potent that all the guards would leave him for the next two hours, and, here, as he would climb into this pool of human waste all alone, he would begin to sing,

> I come to the garden alone,
> while the dew is still on the roses,
> and the voice I hear, falling on my ear,
> the Son of God discloses,
> and He walks with me and He talks with me,
> and He tells me I am His own,
> and the joy we share as we tarry there,
> none other has ever known.

C. Austin Miles

Once you have established your private time with the Lord, it will be easier to pray during your daily tasks. As the prophet Isaiah said, our Christian life is line upon line, precept upon precept, and prayer upon prayer. Take the opportunity to pray during these times that require less concentration, like ironing, gardening, walking, waiting on the phone or the plane, and, as you do so, you will find that your life will be built around prayer *rather* than prayer around your life.

Someone once said, 'God is original in each of our redeemed personalities'. Trust Him to lead you into a life of prayer until you have learned to 'pray without ceasing'.

Look at David, King of a nation, with responsibilities from morning till night, and, yet, he says, 'Everyday I will bless you' (Ps. 145:2). 'My soul waits for the Lord more than those who watch for the morning' (Ps. 130:6 KJV), '. . . at midnight I will rise to give thanks unto Thee' (Ps. 119:62). 'My heart also instructs me in the night seasons' (Ps. 32:8 NKJV). David had learned to pray at all times despite his heavy schedule. The problem is not the lack of time, it is our unwillingness to pray.

When David was organizing the activities of the Temple, prayer, praise, thanksgiving and sacrifice unto the Lord were the primary functions. From morning 'til evening the Temple was filled with ministry unto the Lord, and this is now a picture of us as individual temples of the Holy Spirit. Jesus said, 'My house shall be called a house of prayer' (Mt. 21:13 KJV), and that refers to us as much as it did to the synagogue. We must leave the hustle-bustle of life, drive out the money changers and draw nigh unto God.

Chapter 9

Practical Hints

How to Desire to Pray

With great joy and God's grace, I am able to say, 'I want to pray!' For some this is a great mystery, for others a source of frustration, but the gift of 'desire' is for all.

The Israelites were unable to keep the law because the law was not in them. But today we have a new covenant. Hebrews 8:11 (NKJV) says, 'I will put My laws in their minds and write them on their hearts; and I will be their God, and they shall be My people'.

It is the Holy Spirit who lives within us that gives us the desire to pray. 'God is working in you both to will and to do for his good pleasure' (Phil. 2:13 NKJV). Isaiah said, 'Every morning he makes me eager to hear what he is going to say to me' (Is. 50:4 TLB).

But you ask, 'how do I get this desire to pray?' Beloved, if you are born again and the Holy Spirit lives in you, then you *have* the desire. It is in there, but it may be just a seed, and because it is a very small seed, you may not be aware of it.

I can remember when I first felt this desire to pray. The more I responded to it, the bigger this 'wanting-prayer' seed grew. Now I am very aware of the Holy Spirit calling me to prayer. In the beginning it was hardly noticeable, but as I began following the leading of the Spirit, my seed grew.

Have you not felt the desire to pray from time to time? Even as you have read this book, you may have sensed the 'wanting-prayer' seed of the Holy Spirit in your spirit. As you respond to that inner sense, your prayer seed will grow into a giant 'wanting-prayer' seed called 'praying without ceasing.'

At that point your 'wanting-prayer' tree will begin dropping seeds into other people, inspiring them to pray, which is what this book is, a 'wanting-prayer' seed.

All that God does begins with seeds. Jesus was a seed in Mary. The entire human race was in the seed of Adam. The plan of redemption was a seed in God's heart. Nothing is instant in God's Kingdom. So begin to water that 'wanting-prayer' seed now, and watch it grow.

Prayer to Action

A common mistake made by Christians is that they walk by feelings rather than God's word. It is the difference between obeying one's five physical senses or one's spiritual senses, the old nature versus the new nature.

While in prayer Christians will have many wonderful experiences with God but once they have left their prayer closets those experiences fade away, and doubts, fears, and the circumstances of life crowd in, causing them to question what God did or said while they were in prayer.

Some will seek God for guidance and while in prayer God's voice will seem so clear and plain that great joy will fill their hearts as they arise with the light of glory on their faces. Yet when it comes time to obey and actually step out on God's Word, doubts and contrary circumstances will loom up in their path and they will conclude that it was not God who spoke to them.

Others may experience great faith. God will rise up within them and they will feel as though they could slay a lion, climb any mountain, crush demons. In that moment all things will seem possible. Yet when the 'feelings of faith' are gone, they will discount their experiences and think they no longer have any faith.

When we experience God in prayer, we need to understand that this is TRUTH, and when the world, the flesh, or the devil speak contrary to God, that is untruth.

When Paul was on the ship going from Myra to Rome, he

was caught in the midst of a disasterous storm. They lost control of the ship and the wind was driving them where it willed. They had not seen the sun or stars for 14 days which kept them from knowing where they were and where they were heading. Fear was on the lips of every man. So fierce and unrelenting was the storm that death seemed imminent.

Yet Paul was praying. And soon the answer came. An angel appeared to him and said, 'Fear not, Paul, thou must be brought before Caesar: and lo, God hath given thee all them that sail with thee' (Acts 27:24 KJV). What a prayer experience! What a word from God! What an answer to intercession!

But did he dare ACT upon the word he received? Yes! He stood up in the midst of the storm, in the very face of death, and boldy stated to all on board, 'Wherefore sirs, BE OF GOOD CHEER: for I BELIEVE GOD, THAT IT SHALL BE EVEN AS IT WAS TOLD ME'. Paul put feet to his prayers, he *acted on* what he received in prayer.

When the angel was standing next to him speaking God's Word, Paul was no doubt caught up in the presence and awe of God. But when the angel left, the sensations of the storm came rushing back again. What was he to believe? The answer must always be GOD and His WORD!

Prayer is a two-sided coin – one side spiritual, the other side practical. When John was in the Spirit on the Island of Patmos, he had a vision of Jesus Christ as few men have ever had. Yet when the vision was over, he still had to write down the message he received and give it to the churches.

When Isaiah saw Jesus high and lifted up, with His glory all around, his practical response was to go and preach.

God speaks to us in prayer because He wants us to respond. Moses made the tabernacle because he received the instructions in prayer. Solomon built the Temple because David received the blueprint in prayer. The building, however, was very practical. It took muscle, money and endless logistical details to work out the prayers of Moses and David.

What has God said to you in prayer? Have you been caught in the battle between faith and doubt, Spirit and flesh, God's word versus circumstances? Do not despair!

Just 'take it to the Lord in prayer', and He will speak the word to you again. He will revitalize the vision, strengthen your heart and confirm His direction. The Father knows that 'faith cometh by hearing and hearing by the word of God'. He does not mind repeating Himself. Simply stay in prayer until you have accomplished all that he has spoken to you! This is the difference between success and failure!

Words

The words we speak in prayer are important. Solomon said, 'Death and life are in the power of the tongue . . .' (Prov. 18:21 NKJV). We can either diminish or increase our prayer life simply through the words we speak.

Have you ever talked yourself out of praying? Have you ever complained or murmured while in prayer? Such discouraging words will discourage your faith, dampen your desire to pray or even change your image of God from who he really is to your own word description. It is one thing to pour your heart out to God. It is another thing altogether to gossip, criticise and belittle through prayer. Paul warns us saying, 'Be not deceived, God is not mocked: for whatever a man soweth, that shall he also reap' (Gal. 6:7 KJV).

When Elijah was threatened by Jezebel he prayed his complaint asking God to take his life. God answered and Elijah was translated to heaven, but because of this prayer (which was prayed from the flesh and not the spirit) Jezebel, a demon-possessed woman, ruled over God's people for another ten years. Elijah's words had a very negative historic impact!

This is why praise is so important in prayer. Many of David's prayers began with words of discouragement and anger but ended with words of triumphant praise. Praise inspires life, joy, exhuberance and a positive attitude. You cannot complain while praising! David wrote, 'Whoso offereth praise glorifieth me: and to him that ordereth his conversation aright will I show the salvation of God' (Ps. 50:23 KJV).

Ordering our words in praise opens the door for God's salvation to enter our situation. What a difference this salvation could have made for Israel had Elijah ordered his conversation aright with the Lord!

James very pointedly describes the power of our words when he writes, 'Even so the tongue is a little member, and it can boast of great things. See how much wood or how great a forest a tiny spark can set ablaze! And the tongue is a fire. The tongue is a world of wickednes set among our members, contaminating and depraving the whole body, and setting on fire the wheel of birth – the cycle of man's nature – being itself ignited by hell (Gehenna)' (James 3:5–6 AMP).

Words can determine destinies. When our tongue has been set on fire by hell it produces hell on earth. But when inspired by the Spirit it produces heaven on earth. Words give authoritative access to God or Satan. This is why Paul instructs us to yield our bodily members (which includes our tongue) as instruments of righteousness and not as instruments of unrighteousness.

Prayer is a perfect time to practice ordering yours words, to learn to control your tongue. Before 'speaking your mind', speak in other tongues or quote scripture. This will give the word and the Holy Spirit time to fill you with the mind of Christ. In this way you can pray the will of God rather than the will of the flesh or even the devil.

Guidelines for Prayer

When we pray, we should have specific ideas of what God wants us to pray about and what we need to pray for. There are times, especially during intercession, when God sets the prayer agenda, but, in general, boundaries and guidelines are needed for productive prayer time.

Jesus dealt with this issue when He gave His disciples a model prayer known as the Lord's Prayer to help them order their prayer life.

First, begin with a time of praise and thanksgiving. Tell the Father how much you love and appreciate Him. One song writer said, 'Count your blessings'. David said over 300 times in the Psalms, 'Praise the Lord'. Paul said, 'Rejoice evermore', and 'in everything give thanks: for this is the will of God in Christ concerning you' (1 Thess. 5:16,18 KJV). Praying, singing, shouting, or whispering one of the Psalms are all beautiful ways to begin your prayer time.

Praise will often move into worship, as God begins to fill your soul. Here in worship the awe and wonder of God bows our hearts and knees before Him. He becomes our total consciousness. As David said, 'O come, let us worship and bow down: let us kneel before the Lord our maker. For He is our God' (Ps. 95: 6–7). This is your opportunity to acknowledge God as God, to revere with deepest love His Glory, Sovereignty and Holiness.

In this place your mind, soul and body become still before God. You 'have calmed and quieted (your) soul, like a weaned child with his mother, like a weaned child is (your) soul within (you) (ceased from fretting)'' (Ps. 131:2 AMP). This is a good place to meditate upon God and His word. Take an attribute of God or a verse from the Bible and think upon it, ponder it, mull it over in your mind until the Holy Spirit gives you light concerning it. Then let the thoughts of God flow from His Spirit through your mind.

From here your prayer may take many turns, depending on what God has revealed to you. You may burst into a time of praise and thanksgiving again, or feel the need for personal repentance. Your spirit may be quickened to interced for someone, or a response of a deeper commitment may be in order. An answer you have been seeking may come, and the time to claim the promise in faith should be seized.

Following on, we are instructed to 'ask'. Bring your needs and desires before the Lord. Be specific and clear. There is no need to hem and haw, 'for the Father knows what we need before we ask' (Mt. 6:8). This is called the prayer of petition. When a lawyer petitions a court, he knows what to ask, we must know also. Vague prayer produces vague answers. Specific prayers receive specific answers.

Now it is natural to continue petitioning God for others. The whole world is in need, and you have the privilege and right to beseech God on its behalf. Pray for your family, friends, neighbours, fellow students or employees, the body of Christ, as well as particular members like pastors, evangelists, prophets and apostles, missionaries, teachers, elders, deacons and helpers; people in positions of authoritiy in your community and nation. Then pray for those in other lands. From time to time you will also want to pray for various crises and disasters throughout the world.

There is no need too small or too large. After all, God created a world full of details. If you need a list, make one. I carry a computer list of every name on our mailing list, so I can name their names before the Lord. Lists are a very useful tool in effective praying.

Your prayer time is just about over; now you can end with a time of praise once again. Why praise? Because it is a key to magnifying God and forgetting ourselves, to keeping our gaze ever up and not downward, to expressing unashamedly our love for Jesus Christ our eternal Lord.

This has been only a cursory description of one suggested format for prayer, a private time with God. The key is to be taught and led by the word and Spirit. For in this way our prayer life will not become rigid, formal, boring or religious. God is creative, inventive, and desires us to be adventuresome. Many a time when I enter into prayer, I find that a whole hour or more is filled up with just praise or intercession, speaking in other tongues or meditation. I look forward to private prayer because I know God has new surprises and ventures yet unknown to me.

Delight yourself also in the Lord,
And He shall give you the desires
of your heart.

(Ps. 37:4 NKJV)

Concentration

There are many who put their time into prayer but when they are through they are the same, not having ever really broken through to God. This makes prayer a difficult task and a laborious exercise.

79

However, there is a place where we *can* break through, enter into His presence and touch Him, where we have drawn nigh unto God and he has drawn nigh unto us. Once we have broken through the natural into the spiritual, prayer takes on a whole new dimension.

This requires concentration. It is focusing your spirit, soul and mind on the Lord as well as reaching out to Him in expectant faith. Whether your prayer involves meditation, praise, petition or intercession, concentration is required to enter into the sanctuary with God.

Do not give up too quickly because the more you practice the quicker you can enter in until you are walking in His presence continuously. Be prepared to deal with the obstacles that would separate you from God. As you break through in prayer your spirit, mind and body will be riveted on the Almighty. You will gain a great desire to remain focused on Him and will want to return to this place time after time, a great incentive as you increase your ability to concentrate on the Master!

Chapter 10

A Surprise
The Cost and Time of Prayer

In dealing with the practical side of prayer there are two words that, on the surface may appear negative, but when viewed from God's perspective, they reveal a dimension of divine splendour. These words are *time* and *cost*.

To be honest, there *is* a cost of prayer, and the salient cost is time. Obviously this is one of the reasons why Christians do not pray more. They have not yet experienced the majesty and all-embracing wonder of God. They are judging prayer from outside of the Veil, where the carnal mind cannot comprehend the things of God.

It takes time to get alone with God, to quiet the mind and soul, to still the body and overrule spiritual distractions in order to break through into God's presence. David said, 'Surely I have calmed and quieted my soul, like a weaned child with his mother; like a weaned child is my soul within me' (Ps. 131:2 NKJV). Once we are quiet, His voice is clearer and our perception keener. We can then receive the spiritual things of God more readily.

Daniel prayed three times a day, morning, noon and evening. His prayer time was a great cost to him. He was a prominent governmental official with numerous responsibilities. He had many demands, pressures, decisions and red tape to work through. Yet he found time to pray.

God honoured Daniel and he gained favour. He began to have a godly influence upon an ungodly nation which became a threat to Satan's plans. Soon his prayer time was challenged, and he was forced to make a decision between prayer and compromise, prayer and death. Satan struck at the heart of Daniel's spiritual power: prayer. And what was Daniel's response? Prayer!

This act of faith and faithfulness not only miraculously delivered Daniel but also destroyed his enemies and brought Daniel greater honour, all because he refused to be cowed by Satan's threats and pressures on the job. To Daniel time with God was more valuable than his very life.

Jesus said in Matthew 16:25 (NKJV), 'For whoever desires to save his life will lose it, and whoever loses his life for My sake will find it'. This life means soul life, your personal fleshly life. It is laying down your will, desires, wants and thoughts, your personal preferences and activities. You must surrender your time, energy and leisure, allowing them all to be replaced with Christ's life and will. This exchange can be accomplished in no greater way than in prayer.

Daniel layed down his soul life to find Christ's life instead. He could have rationalized and made excuses, but for Daniel there was no way out of prayer. It was his way of life.

Cost and time are only relative to our needs, desires and demands. Once these three things are in order, cost and time take on a completely different meaning. In the light of the Eternal Christ, the significance of cost and time diminishes, but in our everyday lives, they can become a tyranny. It all depends on what our priorities are in life.

When I was completing my graduate work at a university in Southern California, I would often see surfers in the water before 6:00 am as I drove to the campus for prayer. To them surfing was not costing them anything or taking time away from other activities. It *was* their activity, it was their choice, it was their life. So prayer is to be for us.

It is not a matter of choosing prayer over other activities or feeling as though we are missing out on something better. These feelings occur only when we first start to pray, and it does seem as though it is costing us everything. However, as prayer becomes a way of living, cost and time will take on a divine splendour.

Like all the prayer warriors of the past, you will learn that spending much time in prayer will increase your productivity. Your strength will be renewed, your mind quickened. Your life will become more organized because the fruit of temperance (discipline) will be developed. Your daily activities will be sparked with a divine energy and wisdom, creating greater efficiency and competence.

Seeing it God's Way

Breaking through in prayer allows you to see time as God sees it, eternally. In God it does not matter whether we are in prayer for a moment or for hours, all that matters is that we are in God. We learn as Isaiah did that 70 years is but a moment, and like Peter, a thousand years a day.

Our lives are but a breath in the plans of the Alpha and Omega, The Beginning and The End. In prayer His ways become our ways and His time our time. God's way was 30 years of preparation and three and a half years of ministry for His Son, yet His ministry is eternal. David, Moses and John the Baptist all spent many years in the desert, but they did not consider it wasted time. Because of their prayer life their ministries are still affecting millions of lives today.

Behind the scenes of every great ministry, miracle and move of God is years of prayer. From Genesis to Malachi, 4,000 years of prayer were prayed for the birth of Christ. From the Apostle Peter to you and me, almost 2,000 more years of prayer have gone up for Christ's return.

As we begin to understand this, we will not make the same mistakes Israel did who knew only the acts of God; but like Moses we will know the ways of God. We will understand that prayer precedes ministry. God's ways of time are all-sufficient for answered prayer.

While in prayer on the Isle of Patmos, the Apostle John was found 'in the Spirit'. In this realm he saw the future as present, the end as already accomplished. In God's mind, all that John saw was already an established fact even though it had not occurred in our time realm. God said to John in Revelation 21:6, 'It is done'. In God's realm, He called those things that are not yet as though they were. In Revelation, chapter 19, John both heard and saw you and me in heaven. We were thundering, 'Alleluia! For the Lord God Omnipotent reigns!' (Rev. 19:6 NKJV). And he saw us 'in the armies of heaven, clothed in fine linen, white and clean, following Him on white horses' (Rev. 19:14 NKJV). Was not the faith of John set ablaze when he saw the Church, which he had been praying for, victorious and all-glorious. He saw the Church as God sees it because prayer lifted him into God's time.

When God wants change, He speaks the desired result, not what he sees. He called Abram Abraham, which means 'the father of many nations', before he even had a son. He called Gideon 'a mighty man of valour' when Gideon saw himself weak and small. God anointed David King of Israel when he was just a boy watching sheep. When God looked down on planet earth and saw it dark and void, He said, 'Let there be light', and it was so. If He had spoken what He saw, nothing would have happened.

When our prayers enter into God's realm, we will speak as He speaks, *the answer*! No longer are we bound by what we see or feel. Ephesians 1:3, 1 Corinthians 3:20–23, and 2 Peter 1:3 all tell us that God has given to us all things. 2 Corinthians 1:20 says that God has also said 'YES' to all He has promised us. God is NOW, His answers are NOW. Thus, our prayers must become NOW in God.

This can be seen in the classic example of Daniel. He had prayed for 21 days, and when the angel came to give him the answer, he said, 'For from the first day that thou didst set thine heart to understand, and to chasten thyself before thy God, thy words were heard, and I am come for thy words.' (Dan. 10:12 KJV). God had answered him the first day, but the evil spirit of Persia hindered the angel for 21 days from bringing the answer to Daniel.

God is now, and all that we need is available now. It's only in the receiving that time is involved, because when the answer comes from heaven to earth there are obstacles, such as Satan's kingdom, doubt, ignorance or sin. Daniel persevered because his prayer life was caught up with God, and he could see the end result.

From this perspective then, cost and time lose their relevance. For Daniel and these other men, prayer was life's occupation, and all else sprung out of it. They saw that prayer is the very mechanism that releases God's Kingdom into mankind's history. Failing to pray is what costs the most. Whole generations can be lost, as during the Dark Ages, through prayerlessness. History waits and calls for the prayers of God's people. Can we not afford to lay down our life for God's love to rescue wandering humanity?

TIME WITH YOU

I was busy, running here and there,
Filling my life's dream and all its care.
Piling up things, new houses and treasures,
Looking for acceptance from the world.
But thieves broke in — rust marred the treasure
Gone were the things that brought much pleasure.

Time with you will never pass.
The moments spent with you will always last.
You give me things from eternity.
And I will spend my time with you.

What is life? But a vapor,
A puff of smoke, a mist that disappears.
As for man, his days are as a flower.
He blooms, then just withers away.
Nothing lasts forever — all will burn with fire,
But time with you will stand eternally.

Seeking things above and God's way that is right
Storing up riches far beyond.
Working in the Kingdom, fighting the good fight,
The dawning of His glory is now in sight.

Time with you will never pass.
The day of your appearing will come at last.
I will reign with you eternally,
And I will spend my time with you.

Trina Hankins

Chapter 11

Prayer and the Human Body

Our bodies were created for the Lord, 'Now the body is not for fornication, but for the Lord; and the Lord for the body' (1 Cor. 6:13 KJV). Our union with Christ in the Spirit is to be carried out in a very practical way through our body. His thoughts become our action, His will our motion.

As a child grows accustomed to his body, so must we learn to coordinate our bodies with the mind of Christ. This is where prayer becomes vital, because it serves as a training ground for this spirit-physical interchange.

God created man a three-part being, spirit, soul, and body (1 Thess. 5:23, Gen. 2:7). Our souls were designed to interact with the realm of ideas, thoughts, imaginations and emotions. Our bodies were fashioned to contact the physical world. Since man is a three-divisional being, he has the capacity to take things of the spirit, translate them into understandable concepts in his soul, and then visibly manifest them through the body.

While in prayer, Moses received in the spirit realm the laws, customs, precepts and principles for godly living. Then the Holy Spirit gave Moses revelation knowledge or understanding of these divine thoughts in his mind. Once Moses was able to comprehend them, he began to teach them to the Israelites. This eventually evolved into the Jewish culture, a visible form of spiritual life.

God Visible Through Man

God became visible to man through the incarnation of

Jesus Christ. Certainly there can be no greater display of Divine love than Jesus' intercession on the cross. He physically, as well as spiritually and in His soul, prayed our deliverance.

Therefore, our bodies are of great importance to God and to us, for God's will is worked out on earth in our bodies. You will notice that when your body ceases to function, your stay on planet earth is over; the reason being you have lost that part of you that relates to our physical planet.

The Father prepared a body for Jesus and He used this body to fulfil the Father's will; in this process, prayer played a great part. We see Jesus kneeling (Luke 22:41), raising His hands (Luke 24:50), sitting down (Luke 22:19), standing up (Luke 9:20), prostrate on the ground (Mark 14:35), walking (Mt. 11:20–27), stooping down (John 8:6), and hanging on the cross (Luke 23:34). Jesus brought His body under submission and used it as an instrument of prayer.

For Christians the body is many times the final frontier to conquer. Getting the body into a position to pray is like trying to quiet an erupting volcano. This is because, when we were without Christ, we obeyed the body and trained it to have its own way. Now God has put us back in the driver's seat by the new birth. With Christ in us by the Holy Spirit, we now have the power and knowledge available to us to control our bodies as God originally planned.

Paul writes, 'Do not let sin control your puny body any longer; do not give in to its sinful desires. So let not any part of your bodies become tools of wickedness to be used for sinning, but give yourselves completely to God, every part of you, for you are back from death and you want to be tools in the hands of God, to be used for His good purposes' (Rom. 6:12–13 TLB). Now we can choose who will control our bodies, and we can choose Christ on a continual basis. He helps us retrain them for His glory.

When you wake up in the morning and hear the Spirit calling you to pray, what does your body say? 'No, you're too comfortable and warm. Besides you're too tired and you need your rest'. It is here we must take control of our bodies. As Paul said, 'Like an athlete I punish my body, treating it roughly, training it to do what it should, not what it wants to' (1 Cor. 9:27 TLB). We must do the choosing. We must take the responsibility.

Jesus has now become our High Priest who ever lives to make intercession for us (Heb. 7:25, John 16:26,27), but he is not praying independently of us. Christ the Head is still working in and with and through His body, the Church, to ever intercede. Christ Jesus is praying for us through *us*. We, the Body, are being led by the Spirit to pray for one another as Christ the Head directs. Therefore, we are instructed to 'present our bodies a living sacrifice, holy, acceptable to God' (Rom. 12:1), especially in prayer. If my thumb were to rebel and not cooperate with the other four fingers, I would be limited in what I could do. Likewise, if we refuse to pray, we are hindering the rest of the body. If we do not pray, who will pray in our place? God has called *each* one of us to pray our part and if someone else is praying our prayers, who is praying their prayers?

How important is our body in prayer? When Daniel was threatened with death if he prayed, we see that he went into his room, knelt down on his knees, lifted up and spread out his hands and prayed. Daniel could have prayed in a more secretive manner and no one would have known the difference. But the reason he prayed in the physical posture that he did is because he was obeying the word. 1 Kings 8:44–45,54 (NIV) says, 'When your people go to war against their enemies, wherever you send them, and when they pray to the Lord *toward* the city you have chosen and the temple I have built for your Name, then hear from heaven their prayer and their plea, and uphold their cause'. And it was so, that when Solomon had made an end of praying all this prayer and supplication unto the Lord, he arose from before the altar of the Lord, from *kneeling on his knees with his hands spread up to heaven*'.

Daniel was going to battle so he prayed toward the temple and in the same bodily position as Solomon – which is why God upheld his cause. His bodily position was a statement of faith.

Serious prayer is not done in a lounge chair, although

there are lounge chair prayers. The type of praying will determine our body's position. In worship our bodies will take on a demeanour of reverence. In praise it's an expression of joy and exuberance where dancing, jumping, clapping, leaping, playing of instruments or lifting up of hands is more fitting. In intercession one can experience physically the prayer he is praying.

Paul travailed, going through the labour process of giving birth to churches (Gal. 4:19). Isaiah walked around naked for three years as a symbol of the troubles coming upon Egypt and Ethiopia (Is. 20:1–6). Ezekiel laid on his left side for 390 days and then on his right side for 40 days as a demonstration of what was awaiting Israel and Judah in the way of judgement (Ez. 4:1–6). Hosea married a prostitute and had children by her, illustrating the way God's people had been unfaithful to Him (Hos. 1:2–3).

The cases of Isaiah, Ezekiel and Hosea are unusual and exceptional examples of intercession, but, none the less, illustrate the importance our bodies have in prayer. Truly, these men understood 1 Corinthians 6:20 (NIV) which says, 'For God has bought you with a great price. So use every part of your body to give glory back to God, because He owns it.

> Have thine own way, Lord,
> Have thine own way.
> Thou art the Potter
> I am the clay.
> Mould me and make me,
> After Thy will,
> While I am waiting
> yielded and still
> > George C. Stebbins

Chapter 12

The Challenge

You have now come to a point of decision. 'To pray or not to pray, that is the question!' Reading about prayer, discussing prayer, getting excited or even knowing about prayer is not sufficient. PRAYING IS THE ONLY ANSWER!

The Spirit of the Lord is saying to you even as He said to Israel, 'Ye have dwelt long enough in this mount: turn ye and take your journey, and go . . .' (Deut. 1:6–7). Wherever you are in your prayer life, it is now time to move on. He has set the land before you and has sworn to give it to you. Will you not go up and possess it?

It is in this land of prayer that opportunities and victories await you. It is here that, 'God is able to do exceedingly abundantly above all that you ask or think according to the power that WORKETH IN YOU' (Eph. 3:20).

God has given us the greatest, most life-changing, supernatural, history-making tool known to man – PRAYER. But we must pick it up and go to work. We must turn to the battle on our knees. Individual lives, nations and even future generations are dependent upon and influenced by our prayers or prayerlessness.

The Lord impressed upon me to believe Him for $25,000, an amount we were going to need for evangelization. I shared this with my wife but she found herself unable to agree with me in prayer. I then began to pray for her, asking God to bring us to agreement so that together we could stand in faith.

A few days later a miracle occurred. She was outside

hanging up the laundry when the presence of the Lord suddenly appeared all around her. She looked up into the billowing clouds, shimmering in a deep blue sky which appeared only a few feet from her. She held her breath for a moment, sensing that something awesome and holy was about to happen. Then she asked out loud, 'Lord, what do You want to tell me?' His still small voice answered: 'You are My child'. Tears came to her eyes and she said, 'But Lord, I'm holding back! I only want to serve You! Don't let me fail You, Jesus!' Finally she asked, 'What's wrong, Lord? Where am I lacking?' So gently, lovingly, He answered, 'Finances – you are not believing for the $25,000 I have told you to ask for'. She then asked, 'How can You build my faith?' And the Lord said, 'You must speak out in PRAYER and confess with your own mouth the things I tell you to believe for. You must say you are going to get the $25,000. As you PRAY for it, I will build your faith'. And so she did. She stood in the back yard and said, 'In the name of Jesus Christ, I confess and believe that God through the Holy Spirit is planting seeds of finances now. He is putting it into the hearts of certain men to give us the $25,000'.

When she finished PRAYING she said that faith rose in her heart as she never experienced before. My prayer was answered! Her prayer was answered! Our prayers were answered! We received that $25,000 just a month later. That money was used for evangelism and many lives were changed for all eternity. Prayer not only affects the here and now but the future also. Just think, what would have happened if no one had prayed for your salvation?

Be ready to be used. Be instant in season and out of season, for 'now' I beseech you, brethren, for the Lord Jesus Christ's sake, and for the love of the Spirit, that ye strive together with me in your prayers to God . . . for the world' (Rom. 15:30).

Finally, my prayer for you is:

That the God of our Lord Jesus Christ, the Father of glory, may give unto you the spirit of wisdom and revelation in the knowledge of him: The eyes of your understanding being enlightened that ye may know what is the hope of his calling, and what the riches of the glory of his inheritance in the saints, and what is the exceeding greatness of his power to upward who believe, according to the working of his mighty power . . . That ye might walk worthy of the Lord unto all pleasing, being fruitful in every good work, and increasing in the knowledge of God . . .; And finally that ye be strong in the Lord, and in the power of his might. Praying always with all perseverance and supplication for all saints . . . AMEN

(Eph. 1:17–19, Col. 1:10, Eph. 6:10, 18)

References

The Song, *THE B.I.B.L.E.*, author unknown, public domain.

The Song, *TIME WITH YOU*, by Trina Hankins, used by permission.

Verses marked TLB are taken from *THE LIVING BIBLE* copyright © 1971 by Tyndale House Publishers, Wheaton, IL, used by permission.

Verses marked NKJV are taken from *THE NEW KING JAMES VERSION*, copyright © 1979, 1980, 1982, Thomas Nelson, Inc., Publishers.

Verses marked JBP are taken from *THE NEW TESTAMENT* in Modern English. The earlier edition copyright © 1958 by J. B. Phillips. The MacMillan Company. Used by permission of Collins, London, UK.

O.T. verses marked AMP are taken from *THE AMPLIFIED BIBLE, OLD TESTAMENT*, copyright © 1962, 1964, by Zondervan Publishing House, used by permission.

N.T. verses marked AMP are taken from *THE AMPLIFIED NEW TESTAMENT*, copyright © The Lockman Foundation 1954, 1958.

Verses marked NIV are taken from *THE HOLY BIBLE, NEW INTERNATIONAL VERSION*, copyright © 1973, 1978, 1984, International Bible Society, used by permission of Zondervan Bible Publishers.

If you wish to receive *regular
information* about *new books*,
please send your name and address
to:—
London Bible Warehouse
Po Box 123
Basingstoke
Hants RG23 7NL

Name:...
Address: ....
....
....
....

I am especially interested in:—

Music/Theology/"Popular"
Paperbacks
Delete which do not apply